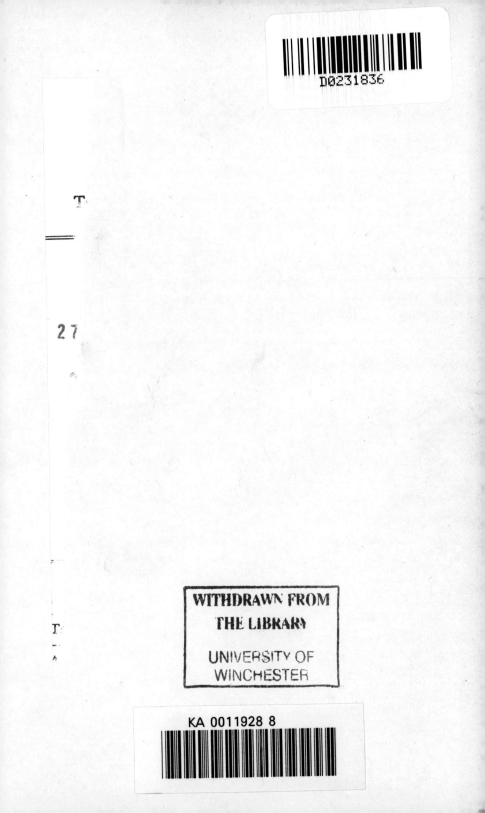

D0231836

T

27

NATIONAL INSTITUTE FOR SOCIAL WORK TRAINING SERIES

NO. 18

ADOPTION OF NON-WHITE CHILDREN

THE EXPERIENCE OF A BRITISH ADOPTION PROJECT

Publications by the
National Institute for Social Work Training
Mary Ward House, London, W.C.1

NO. 1 SOCIAL WORK AND SOCIAL CHANGE
by Eileen Younghusband

NO. 2 INTRODUCTION TO A SOCIAL WORKER
produced by the National Institute for Social Work Training

NO. 3 SOCIAL POLICY AND ADMINISTRATION
by D. V. Donnison, Valerie Chapman and others

NO. 4 SOCIAL WORK WITH FAMILIES
Readings in Social Work, Volume 1
compiled by Eileen Younghusband

NO. 5 PROFESSIONAL EDUCATION FOR SOCIAL WORK IN BRITAIN
by Marjorie J. Smith

NO. 6 NEW DEVELOPMENTS IN CASEWORK
Readings in Social Work, Volume 2
compiled by Eileen Younghusband

NO. 7 THE FIELD TRAINING OF SOCIAL WORKERS
by S. Clement Brown and E. R. Gloyne

NO. 8 DECISION IN CHILD CARE
A Study of Prediction in Fostering Children
by R. A. Parker

NO. 9 ADOPTION POLICY AND PRACTICE
by Iris Goodacre

NO. 10 SUPERVISION IN SOCIAL WORK
by Dorothy E. Pettes

NO. 11 CARING FOR PEOPLE
The 'Williams' Report
on the Staffing of Residential Homes

NO. 12 SOCIAL WORK AND SOCIAL VALUES
Readings in Social Work, Volume 3
compiled by Eileen Younghusband

NO. 14 EDUCATION FOR SOCIAL WORK
Reading in Social Work, Volume 4
compiled by Eileen Younghusband

NO. 15 CHILD CARE: NEEDS AND NUMBERS
by Jean Packman

NO. 16 THE VOLUNTARY WORKER IN THE SOCIAL SERVICES
Chairman of Committee: Geraldine M. Aves

NO. 17 A PLACE LIKE HOME: A PIONEER HOSTEL FOR BOYS
by David Wills

ADOPTION OF NON-WHITE CHILDREN

The Experience of a British Adoption Project

by
LOIS RAYNOR
MA, ACSW

with a Foreword by
SIR FREDERIC SEEBOHM

London
GEORGE ALLEN & UNWIN LTD
RUSKIN HOUSE   MUSEUM STREET

PRINTED IN GREAT BRITAIN
in 11 pt Fournier type
BY UNWIN BROTHERS LIMITED
WOKING AND LONDON

TO THE MEMORY OF
KATE LEWIS TEBBUTT

I have no hesitation in saying that the British Adoption Project is quite an exceptional piece of work. The base for study and action was a ready-made registered adoption society thus ensuring practical experience in the field. Furthermore the Project was located at Bedford College, University of London, where it enjoyed the advantages of consultation with members of the University staff on the research aspects of its work. Very wisely, provision for a co-ordinating service was built in from the start and this led in due course to the formation of the Adoption Resource Exchange which has every indication of becoming a permanent feature in adoption work in Britain, growing into an organization covering an even wider field than the original object of finding placements for the children of coloured parents.

The book is a fascinating human story and although the author modestly remarks 'like so many human studies this one raised as many questions as it answered', it nevertheless succeeds in dispersing whole banks of fog that have so long blurred the adoption picture. For anyone interested in any aspect of adoption, dipping into the book is not enough – it is compulsory and compulsive reading.

The Project's chief conclusion is that children who are of minority race in Britain today *can* find adoptive parents who will love and cherish them. Before the project started many social workers doubted whether adoptions *could* be arranged across racial barriers and many agencies did not feel equipped for what seemed a particularly emotive and risky enterprise. Although the actual numbers of immigrant children needing adoption may not have been large when the Project was first conceived, there is now a growing need with the increased proportion of coloured children in our midst. The probability that there may be changes in the law as a result of the Houghton Departmental Committee on Adoption makes this study especially valuable and timely. The author's criticism of the way some aspects of the law hamper good practice is particularly valuable.

The author, Miss Lois Raynor, as an American social worker with experience in child welfare and adoption, surveys the British scene with a friendly but penetrating eye; she understands both the stresses and the strengths of the British provision. Miss Raynor searches for the basic principles which apply in any setting and she demonstrates that there is a body of useful knowledge about adoption, even though it is not yet possible to establish measurable criteria for predicting success.

Social workers in the local authority social services departments and in voluntary organizations will find much help in Miss Raynor's clear analysis of the basic issues in adoption, the principles which should underlie the work and the way in which knowledge and skill can be applied to this aspect of the welfare of children and families. She highlights the deficiencies which arise from the present fragmentation of provision for unmarried mothers, children available for adoption and prospective adopters; she emphasizes the importance of better co-ordination and of ways of pooling resources to meet the needs of children from minority groups.

The Project was initiated by the concern of Miss K. Luce and the British Branch of International Social Service. The book is dedicated to the memory of Mrs Tebbutt, first Chairman of the Project. Mrs Tebbutt was also one of the first members of the staff of the National Institute for Social Work Training and I am glad to join in paying tribute to the generous contributions she made to many new endeavours.

Much credit is due to those who had the foresight to initiate this Project, to those who have carried it out so ably and to the Foundations which made it financially possible.

ACKNOWLEDGMENTS

The Project described in this book involved the co-operation of many people, and we are grateful to all of them though only a few can be mentioned here individually.

It was Miss Kathleen Luce who first saw the need for the Project while she was Director of International Social Service of Great Britain, and it was she who had the initiative and determination to achieve it. Her idea became a reality through the generous and continued support of five charitable trusts, many local authorities, and several individual donors.

The Adoption Committee of ISS of Great Britain deserves a vote of thanks for its work as the Project's administrative and case committee, and for reading and commenting on this report. As Chairman of the Committee, Mrs Kate Lewis Tebbutt contributed greatly to the success of the work, and, after her death in the final months of the Project, Mr Louis Blom-Cooper kindly served as Chairman.

We are indebted to Professor O. R. McGregor for incorporating the Project into the Sociology Department of Bedford College, and to Professor Margot Jefferys for welcoming us into the Social Research Unit and for providing expert advice to the social work staff in planning and carrying out the inquiries reported here. We are grateful to members of the Project's honorary medical staff, who at that time were all at the Hospital for Sick Children, Great Ormond Street, London – Dr A. P. Norman, Dr Alina Piesowicz and Dr Lionel Hersov – who gave generously and cheerfully of their time and skill.

We wish to thank Professor David Fanshel of Columbia University for the use of his research instruments in the follow-up study, and Miss Jane Rowe, Director of the Association of British Adoption Agencies, for her work in rating the adjustment of the children and their adoptive parents from the findings of that study. We appreciate, too, the splendid co-operation of the staff in the social agencies who worked with us in placing the children and who provided the facts for our national survey.

The most important contribution of all was made by the adoptive parents, and we are grateful to them for cheerfully receiving us into their homes to share their thoughts and feelings at every stage of the adoptive process.

Miss Mary King, of Vancouver, British Columbia, directed the Project for the first eighteen months, and it has been my personal privilege to follow after her and to work closely with my social work colleagues on the staff: J. Newman Hooker, Phillida Sawbridge, Mary Thorne, and Madeline Carriline. Their work has provided most of the material for this book, and in addition they have given encouragement and innumerable thoughtful suggestions during its writing. The work of Barbara Samarasinghe and later Joan Stratford, as office secretary, was essential to the Project, and Jeanne Morley deserves thanks for her careful typing of the manuscript.

LOIS RAYNOR

CONTENTS

FOREWORD   9

THE COMMITTEE   11

HONORARY MEDICAL STAFF   11

ACKNOWLEDGMENTS   13

INTRODUCTION   19

1. ORIGIN AND STRUCTURE OF THE PROJECT
   Original Plans and Later Modifications   25

2. SERVICE TO BABIES
   Sources of Referral and Method of Selection   29
   Characteristics of the Children   33
   Observation and Medical Screening   37

3. THE NATURAL PARENTS
   Experience with Natural Parents   41
   Characteristics of the Mothers: 42
      1. age; marital status, number of illegitimate children   42
      2. religion   43
      3. ethnic background   44
      4. education; occupation and social class; living accommodation   46
   The Decision for Adoption   47
   Characteristics of the Fathers: 50
      1. ethnic background   50
      2. age; health; marital status   52
      3. education; occupation and social class   52
      4. religion   52
   Casework with Natural Fathers   53
   Concluding Remarks   54

4. SELECTION OF ADOPTIVE PARENTS
   Publicity to Recruit Applicants   58
   Pre-application Group Meetings   61
   The First Interview   64
   Subsequent Interviews   67
   Children in the Family   69
   Medical Assessment   70
   Interviews with Significant Relatives   71

The Use of References 72
Handling Rejected Applications 72
Preparation for Adoptive Parenthood 74
Second Child Applications 75
Applicants of Other Races and Cultures 76

5. THE PEOPLE WHO APPLIED TO ADOPT A CHILD
   — A STUDY OF THEIR CHARACTERISTICS
   The Factual Study 83
   1. background; family composition; source of referral 84
   2. age and health of applicants 86
   3. religion; education; employment; socio-economic status 86
   4. applicants' living accommodation and community 89
   5. marriage; size of family; age of children 90
   6. age, sex and race of child requested 92
   7. summary of findings 92
   Principal Reasons for Rejection or Withdrawal 94
   Positive Qualities in Accepted Applicants 96

6. PLACEMENT OF A CHILD
   Choosing a Family for a Child 100
   Parental Consent and Committee Approval 104
   Methods in Placement 107

7. THE PERIOD FROM PLACEMENT TO LEGAL
   ADOPTION
   Supervisory Visits 119
   Experience with 'Welfare Supervision' and the Guardian ad litem 124
   Experience with Adoption Hearings 127

8. POST-ADOPTION DISCUSSION GROUPS
   Purpose of the Groups 131
   Method and Structure 135
   Experience with the Groups 138
   Conclusions from These Meetings 148

9. FOLLOW-UP STUDY OF THE ADJUSTMENT OF THE
   CHILD IN THE ADOPTIVE FAMILY
   Purpose and Plans 151
   Research Method 152
   Report on Follow-up Interviews with Adopters 154
   Rating the Progress of the Adoptions 158
   Summary of Ratings 164
   Plans for Continuing Research 165

10. AGENCY ADOPTIONS OF NON-WHITE CHILDREN IN THE UNITED KINGDOM — A QUANTITATIVE STUDY

Research Method   166
Adoption Orders for Agency-placed Children   167
Foster Home Adoptions   169
Children Not Offered for Adoption   171
Children in Need of Adoption Homes   174
Additional Factors   174
Conclusions   176

11. THE ADOPTION RESOURCE EXCHANGE

Background to the ARE   178
Organization   179
Present Programme   181
Plans for the Future   183

12. CONCLUSIONS AND IMPLICATIONS FOR PRACTICE

Size of the Problem   185
Children and Natural Parents   186
Adoptive Applicants   188
Use of Groups in Adoption   189
Between Placement and Court Hearing   190
At the End of the Project   191

LIST OF MEMBER AGENCIES OF THE ADOPTION RESOURCE   193
EXCHANGE

LIST OF TABLES   194
BIBLIOGRAPHY   196
INDEX   203

B

INTRODUCTION

This is an account of the work of the British Adoption Project in placing more than fifty healthy babies, born in Britain of Asian, African, West Indian or mixed racial parentage, and in studying some of the factors emerging from these placements.

The presence in Britain of an appreciable number of people who are readily distinguished by their difference in colour is a recent phenomenon. Consequently, social workers in this country have had only limited experience in placing children of other races, so that a professional body of knowledge, specifically related to interracial adoption, has not existed in British social work literature. Each worker, when confronted with a request for placement of a non-white child, could draw upon her experience in placing white children, but beyond that she has found it necessary to follow her own personal feelings in the matter and to learn by her own success or failure. This seems particularly unfortunate in work that combines such emotionally charged subjects as adoption and race. It is hoped that the four years of work by the British Adoption Project have made some contribution to the knowledge available on the adoption of non-white children in present day British culture.

Concern for these children, and recognition of the problems the existing agencies found in placing them, prompted International Social Service of Great Britain, in 1965, to create the British Adoption Project in conjunction with the Sociology Department of Bedford College, University of London. The Project was quite unique in its structure, function and setting. It was located at Bedford College and enjoyed the advantages of consultation with members of the University staff regarding the research aspects of the work. As this was the first time a registered adoption society had operated within a university department, we had to examine our goals and methods in order to amalgamate professional social work methods with the academic. This provided a stimulating exercise with results that were very rewarding for the Project, as well as encouraging for any future co-ordinated efforts involving a social agency and a university.

Basically, the Project's assignment was to seek the answers to two questions. Can adoptive homes be found for these children? Will they work out well? This book tells how the answers to these questions were sought within the combined agency and university setting. It considers the service the Project gave to babies, and in some instances to their natural parents, and explains how the adopters were recruited, selected and helped toward adoptive parenthood, as well as the considerations and methods used by the Project in actual placement of the children. An account is given of a study of the characteristics of the consecutive series of couples who applied to the Project to adopt a non-white child. This was an attempt to compare the successful applicants with those who were unsuccessful either because they withdrew or their application was not accepted. The Project's experience in working with adoptive families until an Adoption Order was granted, and the adopters' concurrent experience with 'welfare supervision', the guardian *ad litem* and the various courts are discussed.

Unlike most adopters, ours had to be willing to keep in touch with us until the end of a four-year project and to participate in follow-up studies and discussion groups. We experimented with discussion groups a few months after the Adoption Order was made, hoping to find out if adoptive parents could make use of this method to learn from one another and to gain confidence in themselves as adoptive parents of a non-white child. At the same time we sought to use these meetings to learn how these people felt then about their adopted children and about their experience in applying for a child, as well as to find out if the children's colour was presenting any problems.

One of the original plans was to evaluate the 'success' of the placements at the end of the four-year Project. This was done in follow-up interviews based on a questionnaire designed to assess how well the children and families had adjusted to each other up to that time. We especially wondered if there were any differences in adjustment between the interracial placements and those in which a child had been adopted by people of his own racial background. The most critical period for a child is thought to be adolescence, and this would seem even more true for an adopted coloured child in a white family. Yet we suspect the adjustment in that crucial period may be closely related to the earlier adjustment, especially to the degree of warmth and acceptance enjoyed as a young child in the adoptive family and, a little later, in the way the adopters have been able to tell the child of his adoption and satisfy his curiosity about his natural forebears.

It would be interesting to learn how much the earlier findings were a prediction of later adjustment.

As the work of the Project became known, we received a great many requests, and we began to wonder how many non-white children in Britain were in need of adoption placement. Estimates varied enormously and no one seemed to know how many of these children the voluntary societies and children's departments were being asked to place. We decided to study this situation by research methods and try to learn something about the size of the problem, its geographical distribution and how far the agencies had been able to meet it. We experienced remarkable co-operation from agencies all over the United Kingdom (nearly one hundred per cent) and in 1968 were able to publish a report on the findings of this national survey. They are reprinted here as Chapter 10 with the kind permission of *Race*, the journal of the Institute of Race Relations, London.

The findings of the survey and some experiences we had early in the Project made us aware that adoptive applicants in one area of the country might be waiting, and even become discouraged about taking a non-white child, while children in another area were needing just such a home. There seemed to be an obvious need for co-operation between adoption agencies in bringing suitable adopters and children together and in channelling enquiries through an application centre. An organization on an agency membership basis seemed the most effective way of meeting these needs, and it was decided to set up a nationwide Adoption Resource Exchange.

The English language is not well adapted to writing about race, colour and families in relation to adoption. For instance, there is no really satisfactory word that describes collectively and exclusively people who are of Asian, African or West Indian ancestry. Nor are most English people familiar with the term Caucasian to denote the white race. But the opposite of 'white' is 'black', which is scarcely appropriate for a baby of mixed race, or 'coloured' which offends many people, or 'non-white' which also sounds condescending. In the end it seemed best to use a variety of descriptive words in order, at least, to avoid endless repetition. For the same reason the words 'natural born' and 'biological' children are used interchangeable in distinguishing these youngsters from the adopted children, but neither adjective is really accurate since the adopted children, too, are no less naturally born and no less biological than the others. The term 'extended family' is used here to mean people related by blood or marriage, whether or not they live together in the same household. The feminine pronoun is used in relation to social workers involved in adoptions because of the much larger number of women than men who are engaged in this work.

The forms used in connection with the work of the Project are available upon request at the following places:

National Institute for Social Work Training,
Mary Ward House, 5 – 7 Tavistock Place, London W.C.1.

Social Research Unit, Department of Sociology,
Bedford College Annexe, Peto Place, London N.W.1.

International Social Service of Great Britain,
70 Denison House, 296 Vauxhall Bridge Road, London S.W.1.

CHAPTER 1

ORIGIN AND STRUCTURE OF THE PROJECT

The British Adoption Project grew out of concern about the lack of adoption resources for British-born children of diverse racial origins.

International Social Service of Great Britain knew that English couples had given a warm welcome to Chinese children from Hong Kong. Believing they would do the same for children born here in Britain, iss set up the British Adoption Project to learn what is involved in placing healthy babies of Asian, African, West Indian or mixed racial background in good adoption homes.

To learn as much as possible from this undertaking, it was decided to use research methods to study factors emerging from the placement of fifty to sixty babies. Bedford College became interested, and agreed to take responsibility for the research, while iss, as the Registered Adoption Society, would be responsible for the adoption service. It was hoped the work would supply information about the social work methods and principles in the practice of adoption, as well as facts about adoptive parents and unmarried parents which would be of value to the further development of adoption services generally. The assignment was a large one.

As everyone knows, the decade of the 1950s brought a sharp increase in immigration from Asia, Africa and the West Indies. Included were large numbers of unattached young workers and students resulting in the problem of unmarried parenthood for a few of them. Unmarried English mothers often felt they could not face the future alone with a child of mixed race, while some Asian immigrant mothers were bound by cultural traditions which made a mother and her illegitimate child practically social outcasts. Girls from still other cultures expected their mother to care for the child as was the custom in their home country, but most maternal grandmothers were either far away or they were working outside their home in pursuit of the better life they hoped to find in Britain. The adoption agencies were accustomed to placing English babies with English adopters and found it difficult, if not impossible, to meet the requests to arrange for the adoption of these babies. Consequently, many non-white children were growing up in Children's Homes and foster homes, virtually abandoned by their parents, while others were said to be kept by mothers who felt quite unable to cope and in some cases almost completely rejected them.

At International Social Service there was deep concern for these children and the feeling that something must be done. Perhaps a new adoption agency would be required. Would a temporary project to learn more about adoption for non-white children in Britain help the established agencies develop skill and confidence in this new phase of their work? Unfortunately, there were no figures available to help in planning. No one knew how many of these children needed adoptive families or how many had found them. Figures were not kept by race or colour. Such figures had been unnecessary earlier in a racially homogeneous society, and now some people felt they might be divisive.

An Action Committee was set up by International Social Service to consider the problem, and when a draft project was discussed with a working party of representatives from the Home Office and leading voluntary and statutory agencies dealing with the welfare of deprived children, strong encouragement was given to proceed with the preparation of plans. On December 5, 1962, a Memorandum stated that the purpose of the project would be to provide an adoption service specifically for children in Great Britain, who were of diverse racial origins, and to offer a liaison between agencies to facilitate the adoption of such children. In addition it was proposed to study some of the factors involved in the placements, and to prepare and publish a report of the findings.

Funds were raised and plans laid for a three- to four-year project. In addition to generous individual contributions, grants were received from the Calouste Gulbenkian Foundation, Hilden Trust, City Parochial Foundation, Buttle Trust, Whitbread Trust, and from more than seventy-five interested local authorities.

In March 1965, International Social Service entered into an agreement with Bedford College, University of London, to collaborate in the project, which then became a joint undertaking to be staffed by three full-time, highly qualified social workers with appropriate clerical staff, responsible to the Adoption Committee of the Council of iss of Great Britain. It was agreed that membership of the committee would include people from the college and from iss with the result that it became an advisory committee of professional men and women from related disciplines. Included were three of the staff of the Sociology Department at Bedford College, one of whom, a barrister, was also legal adviser to iss, as well as several very experienced social workers, a paediatrician, a journalist and a former teacher. These specialists brought many different points of view and varied expertise to their task, meeting every four months as a policy group and being on call, as a case committee, to approve placement of children as required under the Adoption Act, 1958.

On April 1, 1965, the British Adoption Project began work with a professional staff of two and an office secretary. A third social worker joined the staff six months later, and during the second half of the Project an additional half-time social worker was employed for the liaison work which by that time had been organized as an Adoption Resource Exchange. Miss Mary King, who was appointed Director of the Project, got the work well under way in the first year and a half, giving particular attention to establishing it firmly within the family of social agencies concerned with child care and adoption. She left in September 1966 and was replaced by the author.

Original Plans and Later Modifications
Those who originated the Project wanted its influence to be spread as widely as possible with benefit to adoption agencies generally, so the staff participated fully in events in the adoption field, giving lectures, talks and seminars, advising journalists and students, and giving consultation to agencies setting up a new adoption service. In the day-by-day work, help and advice were offered in connection with individual children referred to the Project for placement, and to adoption agencies joining the Adoption Resource Exchange. In order not to spread themselves too thin, the staff found it necessary to limit the Project's educational efforts largely to adoption of non-white children. Obviously, the basic principles and methods in adoption apply to all children, but some additional knowledge and skills were found useful in placing children across racial lines and in working with people from different cultural backgrounds.

The research had to be designed to meet academic standards without jeopardizing the value of the adoption service. It was recognized that findings based on the small number of children placed would necessarily be suggestive rather than conclusive. The numbers would be too small to produce more than the most limited statistical findings, so the experience should be studied in depth and every aspect of the work should be documented by detailed records. Some suggested studies had to be abandoned in order to concentrate time and effort on those that seemed most promising as the work developed.

One of the ideas that had to be discarded was a plan to establish criteria for predicting the 'success' of interracial placements. At first glance, this seems simple enough and something every agency would welcome as a blueprint. However, there is incomplete agreement about the qualities necessary to good adoptive parenthood and particularly about the relative importance of each factor. These criteria also are likely to reflect the middle-class values of the social worker and some may be quite irrelevant when applied to people of other classes and cultures. When efforts were made to set up some studies in prediction, it became clear that there were many different life styles into which an adopted child could be assimilated quite happily, but it would be almost impossible to measure these scientific-ally. For example, people adopting across racial lines surely require all the qualities of any good adoptive parents, yet obviously need an even higher degree of genuine acceptance of difference – but how does one measure this kind of variable?

Early in the Project, a comparison group of white babies adopted into English families was planned, but met with many obstacles and had to be abandoned. At first, it was thought the Project might establish such a group, but it soon became clear that this would require additional staff and funds. Then attention turned to forming a comparison group in the children's department of one of the London boroughs, until exploration showed that a busy local authority office, with limited experience of direct adoption placements and harassed by staff shortages and frequent staff changes, would be unable to synchronize its placements with those of a small specialized project such as ours. Nor was any single office likely to have enough infants for adoption to be able to work within the time limit. When these difficulties arose in establishing an external comparison group, it was decided that the Project adopters who were of the same racial background as the children could constitute a small internal group for comparison with the Project's larger group of interracial adopters.

The Memorandum of December 5, 1962, referred to earlier, stated as a fundamental principle that children should be placed whenever possible with adoptive parents of the same racial background as themselves. Yet it had been assumed that most of the applicants would be English families, as people from other lands might need longer to settle into the British way of life before being ready to accept the kind of formal adoption we know. Applications were studied as they were received and, actually, more than one in five of those who adopted babies through the Project were couples where the husband or both partners had come from Asia, Africa or the West Indies. Most of these applicants had been in Britain a number of years and were well established here. They had been through a period of hard work and adjustment but were ready now to plan for a family. As soon as the staff began to understand the aspirations and values these people had brought with them to Britain, there was no problem about these applicants accepting formal adoption or the study and procedures established to safeguard it, although it was all very different from the *de facto* adoptions they had known.

Originally, the Project expected to accept babies for placement from only one or two selected local authority children's departments, but it did not work out that way, as healthy non-European babies needing placement were not known in large numbers to one or two agencies, but were scattered among many. In any event we wanted to try to find homes for a variety of babies rather than for children from one particular group in one section of London. So in the end the Project accepted children from a great many sources, giving the staff wide contacts with the people most concerned about them, and presenting the staff with a comprehensive picture of the children whom the agencies were finding most difficult to place. It had been planned to place young babies, certainly not over a year old, but as it actually happened many of the babies were several months old when referred to the Project, and in other cases a suitable family was not available for some months after agreement to place the child. So five of the children were over a year when adopters were found for them. Some of the babies would have been known to the Project much earlier if plans had included casework with their parents, but funds for this service had not been budgeted, so babies were accepted only when casework service was being given to the mother by another agency. Again, this had the advantage of wider contacts with the agencies which were struggling with plans for these children, and it provided learning opportunities in both directions.

As the work of the Project moved along, there was increasing awareness that following up the children to age two or three would not be adequate, as the most difficult time for them was likely to be much later. This led to plans for extending the follow-up interviews into the years ahead, making it a longitudinal study of the childhood and adolescence of these children in their adoptive families.

Another phase of the work that was modified very much and put into permanent form was the liaison service, which was written into the Project as early as 1962. The liaison between adoption societies started as the volunteer effort of a committee member, and it developed step by step into Britain's first true Adoption Resource Exchange. This will continue to be at least partially self-supporting and is expected to grow in size and usefulness far beyond the end of the Project.

CHAPTER 2

SERVICE TO BABIES

The focal point in adoption is a child – usually a baby too young to speak for himself – so everything an adoption agency does ought to be in the child's best interest. This involves help to natural parents and adoptive applicants, as well, but the work of the adoption agency will be out of focus if the needs of any of these people are allowed to take precedence over the needs of the child. So we shall consider, first of all, the *children* served by the Project.

Sources of Referral and Method of Selection

No attempt was made to find homes for as many children as possible, but rather to learn from a small number what was involved in placing non-European and racially mixed children in Britain, during the years 1965–69. Since the purpose of the Project was both service and research, we sought to serve the children most in need of homes, although a better defined intake policy might have produced a neater piece of research.

Fifty-three babies were legally adopted by applicants to the Project, and after adoption they were the subject of group discussions and a follow-up study. Two additional baby girls were placed but were reclaimed by their mothers before legal adoption. Over three hundred other babies, who were not placed by the Project, were given varying degrees of service, ranging from a single letter or telephone call to placement with adopters in another part of the country through the Adoption Resource Exchange. Only babies of Asian, African, West Indian or mixed racial background were considered. Chinese, though Asian, were not included unless complicated by the presence of other ethnic strains, because we were told that most agencies had been able to find English families ready to accept a Chinese child.

The Project was studying adoption across racial lines, so it was necessary to set limits based on age and health of the children in order to highlight the role played by racial difference in the success or failure of these adoptions. Hence, the babies who were placed had been medically assessed as being in good health and developing normally, but this is not to say that the older or physically handicapped child cannot find a family. Adoption has come a long way since the days when societies hoped to place perfect babies in perfect homes. A more liberal definition of the adoptable child might be 'the capacity to form a relationship with new parents and develop in a family'.[1] Recent studies have confirmed what adopters have been trying to tell us: that a child with a health handicap can be a well loved and satisfying member of many adoptive families, especially if some improvement can be expected eventually in response to good care and medical aid.[2]

Originally the Project planned to place only babies under a year old, but this was raised to 16 months in order to honour our commitment to three children whose placement was delayed. In addition, two toddlers aged 21 and 24 months, although well over our age limit when referred to the Project, were placed because suitable families were available at the right time and particularly wanted children of this age. Thirty-five babies were placed before they were 6 months old, five of these before 2 months and fourteen of them between 2 and 4 months of age, but as Table 2.1 shows, ten babies were between 6 and 9 months, and three were 9 to 12 months. No babies were placed before 6 weeks because of the provision in the Adoption Act, 1958, which makes inadmissible as evidence any document signifying the mother's consent to the proposed adoption unless the child is at least 6 weeks old. The Project maintained that adopters should not be expected to commit themselves as parents to a baby until the natural mother had made her decision, and had taken this formal step to implement it. In every case, save one, the mother signed her formal consent to placement with the adopters before the child actually went to them, although, of course, this consent could be revoked until an Adoption Order was made. The wisdom of our policy may be questioned since some of the babies might otherwise have been placed earlier, and especially since two mothers still changed their minds and reclaimed their babies. In retrospect, it seems that such a consent, signed months before it can become final, is little more than a statement of intention. *Perhaps a deeper understanding of what this particular child means to this mother would have greater prediction value.* There is need for some change in the Adoption Act to allow a mother to make a final decision whenever she is ready to make it. This is a highly individual matter, and there is no reliable evidence that a late decision is any easier to live with in the years ahead.

TABLE 2.1

Age of Children at Adoption Placement

Age of children	Number of children	
6 weeks– 2 months	5	
2 months– 4 months	14	35 (66 per cent)
4 months– 6 months	16	
6 months– 9 months	10	
9 months–12 months	3	
12 months–16 months	3	
16 months or over	2	
Total:	53	

The Project team believed in early placement, and it would have been possible to place younger babies by having the adopters ready first and then looking for young babies to suit them. This seemed to put the needs of the adopters ahead of those of the children, and at the same time to isolate the Project from the general run of children the agencies were finding hardest to place. As it was, some consideration was given to all requests for placement. This resulted in a good deal being learned about the non-European children, who were being offered for adoption, and about the attitudes and methods of the workers, who were trying to give casework service to the mothers of the children.

Over a two-year period, inquiries were received about the possibility of placement for 362 babies, largely from London and the Home Counties. Over 70 per cent of the inquiries were almost evenly divided between moral welfare workers and child care officers in local authorities. A few inquiries came from relatives of the child, but most of the others came from hospitals, local authority health departments, and mother and baby homes.

As might be expected, a wide variation was apparent in the casework skills offered to mothers who were planning for their own and their babies' future. Since the Project could place only a limited number of children, we asked social workers referring babies to the Project to explore with us whether adoption was the only good solution for this child, what resources there were for placement, and what the alternatives to adoption would be. Most workers were eager to learn more about adoption in general, and how to apply this knowledge to placement of children of other races. They felt very unsure of themselves in helping immigrant mothers from different cultures and English mothers of mixed-race babies. Often they worked alone or with colleagues as inexperienced as themselves in this phase of the work, so they welcomed a chance to discuss it.

A few workers hoped for an immediate 'yes' or 'no' answer, seeing the solution to the problem quite simply in terms of any home that might be willing to take a coloured child. These were easily discouraged and ready to report to the mother that no home was available, and that she must keep the child herself or look forward to his being brought up in care of her local authority. However, many more workers refused to admit defeat, and were prepared to take endless trouble to see that adopters were found for the baby.

Some workers requesting adoption for a child had known the mother for months and had a good deal of information about her and the baby. Unfortunately, too few had been able to gain much insight into what this whole experience meant to a particular mother in terms of her personality needs. Such understanding could have been of real help to mothers trying to make a decision that would be right for them. Very rarely was the putative father recognized as a person to whom this experience had meaning, and almost no attempt was made to give him any service. Sometimes he was seen as a source of financial help to the mother, particularly in paying fostering fees for the baby, and sometimes as a person who might threaten the adoption plans by exercising his legal right to apply for custody of the child. There was a tendency to accept too easily the mother's first statement that she was not seeing the father any more, or that he had deserted and could not be found. In taking a medical and social history, the facts on the mother and her family were sometimes judged sufficient, as though a child might not be expected to inherit any characteristics from a missing father.

Sometimes adoption placement was sought before the race of the child was known or the child had been seen, the baby being described simply as 'coloured' of 'half-caste'. There was confusion regarding babies with a parent from countries like Kenya, Guyana or the West Indies, with their multi-racial populations, the assumption being that the person was a Negro when, in fact, he was found to be of Indian or Chinese ancestry. The importance of this sort of information to adopters and expecially to the child himself in later years cannot be over-emphasized.

There was considerable well-meaning but very confused thinking among some of the people responsible for work with unmarried parents or for arranging adoption for babies. There seems a great need for more interchange of ideas and experience, so that what knowledge there is can be available to all. The following examples show the variation we found among agencies and, particularly, the isolation which caused workers to rely upon their own personal feelings and traditions.

One worker said she expected the parents of unmarried mothers under sixteen years of age to take the baby home, while older mothers (and presumably the grandparents) might be permitted some choice in the matter. Some officials tried to discourage mothers from giving up their babies for adoption by refusing care to the child until an adoption could be arranged. In the case of a non-white child this might well be several months, during which the mother would have to care for the child herself, increasing her guilt and conflict until she could no longer relinquish the child even though this might be the best plan for both. A letter from a white worker sought only a coloured family for an African child, saying she did not believe in these children being placed with English adopters as she feared they might not be treated well. By contrast, another worker moved a medium-brown-skinned toddler from a temporary foster home into a residential nursery, rather than consider a rather dark West Indian Negro couple as parents for the little girl because one of her natural parents was white.

Characteristics of the Children

Various facts were made available to us about the children whom agencies were seeking to place, but these were complete only for the twenty-two boys and thirty-one girls, who were adopted through the Project. It is not possible to give the number of each sex referred to us, because 94 (mostly written requests) out of the 362 either did not mention the sex or the child was unborn. In fact, the anxiety of workers faced with placing a non-European child came through in their tendency to refer to the child simply as 'coloured', forgetting all the other characteristics so important in selecting a family for the baby.

Among the requests there were two-and-a-half times as many children with one white and one non-white parent as there were

c

children who were fully coloured. However, from these requests the Project placed very nearly equal numbers, i.e. twenty-five fully coloured and twenty-eight with one white parent. Statistically, children were considered by the Project as fully coloured even when both parents were of mixed ancestry. The racial composition of the Project children is shown in Table 2.2, where it can be seen that nearly two-thirds were Asian or Eurasian, and a little over one-third were fully or partly Negro. Negro and Negro-European children, largely West Indians, made up a larger percentage of the children referred for placement in 1967 and 1968 than they had earlier. This does not necessarily reflect a change in the number of children of different races seeking adoption. It may well be related to the Project's willingness to try to find homes for whatever children were needing it most, as well as the increasing success of adoption agencies generally in placing Asian babies, particularly girls. Towards the end of the Project some approved applicants had to wait several months for a Eurasian baby girl, as agency after agency told us they were now able to find homes for their Eurasian baby girls.

TABLE 2.2

Racial Background of Children Placed by Project

Asian	16
Eurasian (Asian/European)	18
Negro	3
Negro/European	10
Negro/Asian	3
Negro/Asian/European	3
Total:	53

Three out of five of the children placed were brought to the attention of the Project before they were six weeks old, and more than four out of five before three months. In the total group the proportion referred at these ages tended to be much the same. This would seem to indicate that mothers are making an early decision for adoption and that their social workers are aware of the importance of early placement and are trying to ensure this. Research in child development has shown that the age of the child when he loses a familiar parent figure may be a highly significant factor both in its immediate effect and in later personality development. The effects of separation are thought to be less severe in early infancy before a stable relation-ship has been established with a mother figure, and perhaps most severe between six months and two years when the baby is just establishing these relationships.[3]

It is a matter for real regret that only two out of three of the Project's babies were placed in their permanent homes before six months of age, and so is the fact that twenty-five of the children already had experienced changes of mothering after ten days of age and before finally arriving in their adoptive homes. The Project had no control over these moves, because the children were not in our care until they went to adopters, but delay in finding adoptive parents for them was responsible for some of the babies moving from one temporary foster home to another, or to a residential nursery. Twenty-two babies had been in the care of two different mothers. Two others had experienced life with four different mother persons, and one unfortunate little boy, who was eighteen months old when his mother finally was able to release him for adoption, had lived with her on two occasions and, in addition, had lived in four foster homes and one residential nursery.

This last situation was particularly unfortunate as the mother had sought adoption for this youngster as a young baby, but an adoption society had urged her to keep him because they saw little hope of adoption for a West Indian child. Probably the adoption society records show this as 'Case closed – mother kept child', and they will never know it did not work out that way, as the mother did not return to the same agency. She said, 'They made me feel too guilty.' Instead she found a private foster home, but this was soon closed as sub-standard and the baby moved to a local-authority foster home a long way from the mother, so she found another private foster home closer to her. This foster mother became ill and gave up fostering, so the mother took the baby with her into lodgings until she, too fell ill. In desperation she appealed to her local authority which found another temporary foster home, although the mother again insisted she wanted him placed for adoption so he would have a permanent home. The little boy, by then eighteen months old, was referred to the Project, but even after that he was moved again, this time to a residential nursery just as adoptive parents were about to receive him. Obviously it required very special adopters to overcome the deprivation of this little boy's first eighteen months, and we were fortunate to have such a family.

TABLE 2.3

*Type of Care Babies Received Prior to Adoption Placement**

With mother in lodgings	6
With mother in mother and baby home	15
In local-authority foster home	13
In private foster home	26
In residential nursery	11
In hospital for illness	2
With relative of mother	1

* The total is greater than the 53 children involved because some had more than one type of care.

Table 2.3 shows the type of care the Project babies had received. Grouping local authority and private fostering, thirty-nine of the placements were with foster parents and only eleven in residential nurseries. Eight babies went straight from the care of their natural mothers to their adoptive parents, six of these from a mother and baby home. Thirteen had been in the care of their natural mother (four in lodgings and nine in a mother and baby home) before going to a foster home or residential nursery and ultimately to adopters.

If, as many workers believe, a child's pre-adoption experience is second only to the personal qualities of the adopters in determining the outcome of an adoption, then the number of changes of mothering and the quality of that mothering are exceedingly important. To quote Dr Margaret Ribble, 'Sincere and interested people ask: "Does it affect an infant to be placed temporarily in an Institution; is he disturbed by being 'tried out' in one foster home after another; does it make a difference if several different people care for the baby?" The answer is that it usually makes the difference between a well-adjusted child with a sense of security and a child with behaviour problems.'[4]

Although our contacts with residential nurseries have shown some devoted personnel, one still wonders whether it would not be possible for many more of the babies and toddlers in nurseries to be fostered. Of course, an overcrowded foster home with one woman giving twenty-four hour care to several babies or young children is not really family care, and certainly is not a substitute for a well-staffed nursery in the charge of a competent matron, but we believe a well-chosen foster mother with time to devote to a baby has much to offer until a child can be settled with permanent parents. 'Studies of infants raised in institutions repeatedly demonstrate the harmful effect of maternal deprivation on their emotional, social and intellectual development.'[5] David and Appell's study in 1962[6] found that the affective blandness characterizing many institutional environments means that the children are exposed to little strong positive or negative emotional expression. Multiple caretakers often have little chance to know individual children, with the result that their handling is rarely adapted to the child's unique needs and characteristics. The recent work of James and Joyce Robertson of the Tavistock Institute of Human Relations shows on film the destructive effect on a young child of even a very brief period in residential group care.

Studying the length of time from referral until placement, we found that the largest number of children, fourteen, took between two and three months to place. Eleven of these were Asian or Eurasian and three were full Negro children. Nine were girls, five were boys, and the request for their placement was received any time from before birth to the age of eighteen months. However, ten of these fourteen who were placed relatively quickly were referred before they were two months old.

Seventeen girls and only seven boys were placed after being on referral less than three months, yet two of the three children who took over eleven months to place were girls. The three who took longest to place were Negro or Negro-European, and were brought to our attention at three weeks, two months and four months respectively. So perhaps it could be said that to be Asian and a girl and to be referred at an early age were factors associated with relatively prompt placement. Negro girls and a Negro boy waited longest, though they did eventually find good homes. It is difficult to draw any more definite conclusions from these figures because of such factors as (1) agency staff shortages with resulting delays in transmitting social and medical histories to the Project, and (2) delays in our study of adoption applications.

Observation and Medical Screening
The Project's medical consultant worked with the casework staff to develop the forms used for securing medical and developmental histories on the children,[7] and arranged for a paediatrician at the Hospital for Sick Children, Great Ormond Street, London, to examine each child before a decision was made about adoption placement. This paediatrician set aside time at the hospital once a week for Project

babies. She always wanted to talk with the person actually giving care to the child, but the Project caseworker, who was considering the child for adoption, was also present and sometimes the child care officer or diocesan moral welfare worker as well. Appointment for paediatric examination was made only after a social and health history had been received including the child's ante-natal, birth and peri-natal history. We had thought it would not be worth while to seek information from the parents' general practitioners when so many parents had been in the area only a short time, but this may have been unwise because we obtained rather sketchy medical histories from some parents. The social and medical histories were made available for our paediatrician's use, but were not made part of the hospital records. In several instances a baby was examined a second or third time a month or two later if the paediatrician had any question about his health or development.

Seven of the babies examined by the Project paediatrician could not be recommended for adoption placement at that time for reasons of health or slow development. One of these babies was diagnosed as having Pompe's disease and died a few months later. Two babies had been born very prematurely with one showing increasingly poor development at six months, the other a heart ailment at fourteen months. Four others showed slow development, well below that expected for their age. Two of these slow developers had experienced poor physical and emotional care (one in an over-loaded foster home, the other in a residential nursery), but by the time they began to develop more normally in new foster homes they were well beyond the age to be included in the Project's research. Another appealing little boy of twenty months, with a history of poor response during the peri-natal period and several changes of foster home, was seen by a clinical psychologist, as well as by the paediatrician, and was considered to be retarded enough to require special care. The Project paediatrician also examined four healthy babies whose mothers decided not to offer them for adoption after all, and nine others in good health were not placed by us but by other agencies, or a decision was made by their agency workers to leave them in their foster home on a long-term basis.

As the same paediatrician saw all the babies, a close working relationship developed between doctor and social workers with the result that the paediatrician became well informed about adoption and the social workers became more knowledgeable about babies. As an example of this, the workers learned that many Asian and Negro babies have umbilical hernias which very often disappear after several months or years without any treatment; and the doctor learned that it is not necessary to delay adoption placement until such a hernia has disappeared or been removed surgically, since most adopters are not daunted by a minor condition that can be corrected later or may even clear up spontaneously.

The caseworkers themselves observed each child carefully and encouraged the child's caretaker to do the same, since she was in the best position to see him under a variety of circumstances. Together with the paediatrician's findings these observations made it possible to decide whether the Project could find adopters for this child and, if so, what particular needs should be met by his new parents. Actually, only fourteen children were rejected by the Project specifically for poor health or development, but this factor probably entered into the withdrawal of some of the other referrals. Among the 362 children for whom adoption was requested, eighteen had been born at least one month prematurely, ten were said to show slow development and seventeen had other known health problems. One baby referred before birth was born dead and another died suddenly at nine weeks from a respiratory infection before adoption placement.

In adoption there is always the question of how old a baby must be before one can be sure no congenital disease or handicap will show up. The answer to this is that there is no age at which all the risks can be known, and if adopters were not ready to take risks babies would not find homes. But we do know that babies develop emotional problems while they are growing older in temporary care, and these emotional problems are harder for adoptive parents to bear than most congenital handicaps that just might appear later. A psychiatrist with many years' experience as consultant to a large children's society has said, 'Any programme that does not place children early is running the risk of exposing the majority of their children to the certain perils of late placement, in order to protect the minority from the possible dangers of misplacement.'[8] The Child Welfare League of America, in setting standards for its member agencies, says,

'In general, delays in placement to allow for a longer period of study are not warranted. . . . It can be assumed that many adoptive parents are ready or can be helped to take the same risks as natural parents, and can accept an infant with a medical problem or uncertain prognosis, and do not need to have guarantees of perfect babies. A physical handicap or hereditary condition should not preclude early placement, if the facts regarding the handicap are reasonably well established, and if adoptive parents are found who can accept the child with his difference, handicap or condition.'[9]

REFERENCES

(1) Kadushin, Alfred, *Child Welfare Services*, Macmillan, New York, 1967, p. 505.

(2) Massarik, Fred., and Franklin, David S., *Adoption of Children with Medical Conditions*, Children's Home Society of California, Los Angeles, 1967.

(3) Yarrow, Leon J., 'Separation from Parents in Early Childhood', reviewed by Hoffman and Hoffman in *Review of Child Development Research*, Russell Sage Foundation, New York, 1964, p. 122.

(4) Ribble, Margaret, *The Rights of Infants*, Columbia University Press, New York, 2nd Edition, 1965, p. 4.

(5) Taylor, Ann, 'Institutionalized Infants' Concept Formation Reality', *American Journal of Orthopsychiatry*, Vol. 38, No. 1, January 1968.

(6) Reported by Leon Yarrow in *Review of Child Development Research*, edited by Hoffman and Hoffman, Russell Sage Foundation, New York, 1964, pp. 99 and 100.

(7) See Introduction for availability of forms used: (1) ante-natal, birth and peri-natal history, (2) child's development and subsequent medical care, (3) report on examinations by Project paediatrician. Forms now recommended by the Association of British Adoption Agencies were not available for use during the Project.

(8) Dr Ner Littner's Discussion of 'A Program of Adoptive Placement for Infants under Three Months' by Helen Fradkin and Dorothy Krugman, *American Journal of Orthopsychiatry*, Vol. 26, July 1956.

(9) *Child Welfare League of America Standards for Adoption Service*, C.W.L.A., New York, 1968, pp. 28 and 29.

CHAPTER 3

THE NATURAL PARENTS

Experience with Natural Parents

As the Project was not staffed to work with natural parents, babies were to be placed only if mothers were already receiving a casework service and were considered to have made a firm decision for adoption. The idea of adoption as a permanent arrangement was emphasized. The Project did not subscribe to the idea that an adoption home is the place to try out the mother's ability to separate from her child, or to bring the putative father to heel, or to see if the agency really feels comfortable about the adopters as parents. These placements had none of the tentative quality or indecisiveness associated with 'fostering with a view to adoption'. The Project placed children with every expectation that they would be legally adopted and grow up as a child of this family. This kind of placement involves a good deal of advance preparation and no uncertainty once the decision has been made. We found most mothers were grateful for the definiteness of the plan and for the milestone that had been reached when they signed their consent before placement, even though they would need to go back over all this experience of unmarried parenthood again some months later to convince the court they had made a final and right decision.

The Project's part in the work with natural parents was intended to be only around adoption: what would be involved for them; the actual process of the placement as carried out in this agency; what the adopters would be like (except for identifying information) in so far as each mother wished to know this; the actual taking of consent. From an unhappy experience with a mother, who decided to reclaim her child just a week before the adoption hearing, the Project realized that the mother's need for casework support during the period between placement of the baby and legal adoption was not always met by her principal caseworker and might have to be met by the adoption worker. Where the tie with the former worker was strong, a mother wanted only fleeting contacts with the adoption worker during this period, but where the earlier casework relationship had been brief or not very meaningful, (as in the case of the mother just mentioned), she needed to look to the adoption worker to sustain her in the decision she had made (with the accompanying sense of loss), and in picking up the strands of her own life to face the future with confidence. In at least two cases putative fathers also needed and were given help during this period.

We did not suggest that the mother should meet the adopters, correspond with them through the agency or receive pictures of the baby from them later on, because all these can be fraught with great anxiety, and for many mothers they make giving up the baby even more painful and drawn out. But for the mother who finds great satisfaction – or in some cases must punish herself – through these means, the agency tried to arrange these with care and with due regard to each mother and each adoptive family as individuals. What is best for one may not be right for another and we tried to be sensitive to the needs and wishes of all concerned.

Characteristics of the Mothers

Before discussing further our experience with natural parents, some information about them may give a clearer picture of these parents who decided upon adoption as the best answer to an unwanted pregnancy. In comparisons between parents of the children we placed and the larger group of children from whom a selection had to be made, it should be remembered that this choice was made on the basis of need, age, health and the availability of adopters. The characteristics of the babies and their natural parents were analysed at the end of the Project.

1. age; marital status; number of illegitimate children

Mrs Margaret Bramall, in writing of the work of the National Council for the Unmarried Mother and her Child, says pregnancy out of wedlock is not really a teenage problem, though the number of such pregnancies has risen sharply in recent years.[1] In the case of the mothers whose babies were adopted through the Project only three were under eighteen years old when the baby was born. Thirty-seven of the fifty-three mothers were between eighteen and twenty-five years of age, and another nine were twenty-five to thirty years old. Four mothers were over thirty. Unfortunately, figures on the mothers' age are not available for the children the Project did not place, so it is not known if the age of the Project mothers is in any way representative of that larger group.

Twenty of the Project mothers were the eldest in their family; eighteen were the youngest and nineteen were in between, so the pregnancy was not associated with family place. Four were the only child of their parents. Thirty-four came from families of four or more children, but nearly half of these were Asian girls where large families are the norm. For seven mothers this was not the first illegitimate child. Forty-eight mothers were single and five were married, one of these to the father of the child. This last was a situation in which the child was conceived before a Muslim marriage, and the parents were returning home, where they said the child would be considered illegitimate and without status.

2. *religion*

Thirty-four of the mothers of the adopted babies considered themselves Christian, but not more than six of these indicated they were practising Christians, and only four asked to have their child brought up in that faith. Sixteen mothers were followers of one of the religions of the East, the largest number being Hindus. One Muslim parent asked that the child not be given to Hindus or Roman Catholics. Only three girls said they had no religion. We cannot speak for mothers of white children, and we do not know the religion of the mothers of the larger group of children not placed by the Project, but it certainly can be said of most of these fifty-three mothers that religion was not an important factor in thinking of adopters for their children. What they wanted was a warm and loving family, people who would love the child for himself.

If many of the English mothers of coloured babies relinquished for adoption are not practising Christians and mothers from abroad are largely adherents of other religions, perhaps it would be well if some adoption societies could reconsider their policy of accepting only practising Christians as adopters for these children, unless the agencies see their role as envangelical rather than as meeting the need of children for homes. We recently heard about a Chinese, Buddhist couple seeking a Chinese baby who could not be considered because the agency only places children with Christian adopters. Another situation came to our attention in which a Greek Cypriot of Greek Orthodox faith could not be considered by several agencies because of religion, in spite of the fact that Cypriot children are considered hard to place and the Greek Orthodox Christians are in communion with the Church of England. Fortunately, the Adoption Resource Exchange was able to direct these couples to agencies more aware of the urgent need of children to grow up in a family. Some of the rules about religious requirements in adoption were made in the days when there were as many as ten or twenty applicants for each baby and most applicants were likely to be practising Christians, but today this situation is very different in those agencies that are trying to serve the needs of a wider group of children.

3. *ethnic background*

Thirty-one of the babies placed by the Project had mothers who had come to Britain from fifteen different non-European countries around the world. The other twenty-two children had English or Irish mothers. This is a higher proportion of non-European mothers than was found in the total group of 362 mothers. Twenty-six of the Project's mothers were Asian or Eurasian. The large number of children of these mothers selected by the Project may have been due in part to the deep rejection of illegitimacy in most Eastern cultures, which made it virtually impossible for many of these girls to keep their babies and led them to an early and firm decision for adoption. There were only five mothers of Negro or part-Negro background and one of these was born and raised in England. Time and time again, after an early request for adoption, West Indian mothers decided to keep their babies or have them cared for by a member of their family in line with cultural patterns in their homeland. Almost half the non-European mothers had been in Britain less than three years.

It was always necessary to consider the culture of the specific group from which the girl came, remembering the very different attitudes of the religions and cultures of the East from those of the African countries, Guyana and the West Indies and even the cultural patterns of different social classes. The Indian and Pakistani girls, and any others who were Muslim or Hindu, felt their pregnancy outside of marriage was the utmost disgrace. Few could tell their mothers and almost none could tell their fathers, from whom they often said they feared violence in such circumstances. Most of these girls had lived very sheltered lives and had not been prepared to cope with the greater freedom they found as students or young workers in Britain. If their plight should become known they expected loss of status and no chance for marriage. Many girls came from families where their parents were expected to choose their husband, and they wanted to do nothing to upset the plans their parents had made for them.

TABLE 3.1

Ethnic Background and Country of Origin
of Mothers of 53 Adopted Children

Ethnic background	Country of origin	No. of mothers
Indian	India	6
	Trinidad	5
	Guyana	2
	Kenya	2
	Tanzania	2
	Jamaica	1
	Pakistan	1
	Uganda	1
Indian/European (Portuguese)	India	1
Sinhalese	Ceylon	2
Chinese	Malaya	1
Persian	Aden	1
Thai	Thailand	1
Negro	Barbados	1
	Ghana	1
	Grenada	1
Negro/Chinese	Jamaica	1
Negro/European	England	1
European	England or Wales	20
	Eire	2
	Total:	53

The West Indian girls suffered from a different situation, and often from a conflict in cultures. They had hoped to better their social and financial condition by coming to Britain and were reluctant to be held back by the care of a child. The customs many of these girls had brought with them permitted a good deal of sexual freedom before settling down to marriage, but their mothers were not ready to take on the care of a baby as they would have done back home, because they were either employed or too far away. Katrin Fitzherbert, in her study of West Indian children in London,[2] explains the unstable family system that has developed among the poorer people in some of the West Indian islands, a result of an earlier slave culture in which the role of the father in the family was very uncertain. She says that illegitimacy is associated with lower class, but the illegitimate child is accepted in that class without moral stigma. Often he is brought up by the maternal grandmother, who first chastises her daughter and sends her away, so the neighbours will think she rejects her daughter's lower class behaviour. Later, mother and daughter are reconciled and the baby comes home. Possibly this may explain why West Indian mothers in London often ask for adoption and then a little later decide to keep the child. Certainly the child born out of wedlock to a West Indian mother is more likely to be welcome in his natural family than such a child born to most Asian or many English mothers, but the employment of women and the upward strivings of the West Indians in Britain make this an undependable pattern of care, and one that cannot be taken for granted.

4. education; occupation and social class; living accommodation

Some of the mothers of the adopted children had received all their schooling abroad. Others had their earlier education there and had continued it in Britain, some coming here specifically to qualify. Three had earned an academic degree and eight had diplomas. Twenty-one were full-time students including eleven in nurses' training. Thus 40 per cent of the mothers were students. We do not know how this large proportion of students compares with those in the overall group requesting adoption, as there are no figures for the larger group.

Among the mothers of the adopted children, the thirty-two who were not full-time students were engaged in a variety of occupations at the time they became pregnant. Sixteen were employed in offices, six in factories and two were nurses. Also included were a physiotherapist, a librarian, a technician, a hairdresser, a shop assistant and a domestic. One woman was a housewife, and one was a young girl who had come recently from India without ever being employed. In an attempt to learn the social class from which the mothers came, we have classified them in Table 3.2 according to the occupation of their fathers, though these, too, may be somewhat misleading in the case of non-European girls because of the different status some occupations may hold in different cultures.

The living arrangements of the mothers at the time the child was conceived were varied. It is difficult to see much connection between

TABLE 3.2

*Social Class of Mothers of 53 Adopted Children
as Determined by Occupation of Mother's Father
(Registrar General's Classification)*

Social class	No. of mothers
I	9
II	18
III	18
IV	6
V	0
Unknown	2

the accommodation and an out-of-wedlock pregnancy for the largest group of girls, the twenty-two who were living with their parents or relatives. However, there were twelve mothers who were living alone and another twelve were in residential accommodation connected with their work or training, usually a hospital. Two other girls were living with friends and two were cohabiting, one with the child's father, the other with a man who was not the father of this child. The remaining three were married and living with their husbands.

TABLE 3.3

*Living Arrangements of Mothers
of 53 Adopted Children*

Accommodation	No. of mothers
With parents	17
With other relatives	5
Alone	12
In residential accommodation	12
With friends	2
Cohabiting	2
With husband (child's father)	1
With husband (not child's father)	2

The Decision for Adoption

The Adoption Act, 1958, ensures the natural mother every opportunity to reverse the decision she has made for adoption. The court official who witnesses her signature often feels it his duty to remind a mother of her right to change her mind right until the time when an Adoption Order has been made, and the guardian *ad litem* usually explores any possible wish to rescind her signed consent. But no provision is made for the mother who knows her own mind and wishes to relinquish finally all claim to her child shortly after his birth.

Some mothers want their child to get settled quickly with adopters, who will be free to commit themselves wholly to him as parents without fear of losing him. Mothers who are sure adoption is the best answer for themselves and their baby may know a later parting will be more difficult, if not impossible; these mothers want to provide for the child immediately and begin to pick up the broken strands of their own lives. To be asked over and over if they are sure they are doing the right thing and if they want to change their minds, only makes it harder for mothers to see the whole experience in perspective and to adhere to what they believe is the best plan.

Reviewing our files we found that thirty-eight mothers, or nearly three out of four, had reached their final decision for adoption before the child was born, and another eight had made the decision before the child was six weeks old. *This meant that nearly nine out of ten Project mothers were ready to give their final consent to adoption by the time the baby was six weeks old*. It is interesting to note that the only mothers who reclaimed their children after adoption placement had not signed their consent until the babies were five-and-a-half and ten months respectively.

It seems hardly a coincidence that Margaret Yelloly[3] in her study of white mothers of illegitimate babies in Gloucestershire should have found that 70 per cent of those mothers who gave their babies for adoption had reached a firm decision during pregnancy and held to this despite the strong maternal feeling and intense desire to keep the child which often followed the birth. These findings seem to indicate that mothers of babies adopted through the Project were no different from other mothers in making an early and definite decision.

We tried to learn if there were any association between an early decision and the race of the mother, her age or the type of agency she had sought for help. All but seven of the Project mothers had some casework service from a local children's department or a moral welfare worker and the incidence of decisions made before the baby was six weeks old is very nearly the same for both, so the type of agency involved did not seem to be related to the time a decision was made.

The age of the mother also made little difference in when she made her decision, except that all four mothers who were over thirty decided on adoption before the child was born. Considering the girls by racial background, Table 3.4 shows that the European mothers and Asian mothers made their decision early, but the three full-Negro mothers decided after six weeks. Interestingly, the two mothers whose ancestry was only partially Negro made their decision before the child was born. The numbers are so small, that one can only conjecture that the three Negro mothers may have found it harder to decide upon adoption since their cultural background favoured keeping the child within the extended family.

TABLE 3.4

Time of Decision as Related to Ethnic Background of Mother

Time of decision	Asian	Eurasian	Negro	Negro and other	European	Total
During pregnancy	17	2		2	17	38
Child under 4 weeks	2				3	5
Child 4–6 weeks	2				1	3
Child 6 wks.–3 months	1		1		1	3
Child 3–6 months	1		1			2
Child 6–12 months	1					1
Child 12 months or over			1			1
Total:	24	2	3	2	22	53

Some research in the United States has found social class the most important background factor in the decision of an unmarried mother to keep or give her baby for adoption. This analysis suggests that the higher the social class, the more likely the girl is to surrender her baby. It also appears 'that the more realistically the situation is faced without disturbing the normal pattern of the girl's family life, the more likely she is to surrender the baby'.[4] These researchers found that the girl who decides to keep her child is often the unrealistic, indecisive girl with poor psychological functioning, who is from a broken home and is living alone. Yelloly's English study, mentioned above, found that 'unstable and emotionally disturbed mothers are more likely to keep their children despite the presence of characteristics which would ordinarily tend toward adoption'.[5] The factors Miss Yelloly found to be strongly associated with the decision to place the child for adoption

D

were most reliably predictive when they occurred together. These factors were 'a negative attitude toward keeping the child on the part of the natural mother's parents, the fact that the putative father was a married man, and that the mother had other children'.[6] Mothers who had been classified as unstable on the basis of their social history tended to keep their babies, despite the presence of these factors normally associated with a decision for adoption.

Whether placing an out of wedlock baby for adoption in Britain is as dependent upon social class as it is in the United States has not been studied so far as we know, but middle-class English girls may feel under less pressure than their American counterparts, because of the less puritanical attitude toward illegitimacy in Britain. It has been thought that better provision for unsupported mothers would result in more girls keeping their babies, but one could not predict this result in the United States if it is those best able to provide for themselves and their children who have been placing them for adoption. Such provision might be expected, however, to ease the lives of the large number of lower-class mothers who often keep their children even under the most difficult circumstances.

Characteristics of the Fathers

Some of the men who fathered the adopted children were rather shadowy figures only described to us by the mother, but others were active in planning for their children. Thirty-seven had their views sought in connection with adoption planning and seventeen of these were interviewed by a social worker. Thirty-two were said to have acknowledged paternity, but ten of these kept their whereabouts unknown while plans were being made for the child's future. Only one man was involved in any legal proceedings arising out of paternity of these children. This father was sued by the girl's parents for breach of promise because the couple had planned to marry but they were prevented from doing so by the young man's parents, who insisted upon an arranged marriage for their son to a girl of his own race and religion. The matter was settled out of court when the girl's parents realized the father was quite as upset by the turn of events as they had been, and that he was anxious to make amends.

1. *ethnic background*

There were only five European fathers and none of them participated in planning for the child's care. There was the same proportion of fathers of non-European background in the adopted group as in the total group for whom placement was asked, but the proportions of Asian and Negro were reversed, with the total group including a larger number of fathers of Negro extraction. Table 3.5 shows the ethnic background and the countries of origin of the fathers of the adopted children.

TABLE 3.5

Ethnic Background and Country of Origin of
Natural Fathers of 53 Adopted Children

Ethnic background	Country of origin	No. of fathers
Indian	India	10
	Pakistan	7
	Guyana	2
	Trinidad	2
	Iraq	1
	Malaysia	1
	Kenya	1
	Mauritius	1
	Uganda	1
Sinhalese	Ceylon	2
Iraqi	Iraq	1
Arab	Egypt	1
Negro	Jamaica	7
	Barbados	2
	Ghana	2
	USA	2
	Dominica	1
	Uganda	1
Negro/Arab	Sudan	1
Negro/European (Jewish)	Jamaica	1
Negro/European (Portuguese)	Canary Islands	1
European	England	3
	Eire	2

More than half the non-white men had been in Britain from three to ten years, but eight had come more recently and three had lived here more than ten years. In four cases this information was not known to us, and there were five fathers who were still overseas, the mother's pregnancy having started before she emigrated to Britain. Several of the others were said to have returned home during the mother's pregnancy or shortly after the birth of the baby, but in some cases this statement could have represented the wish of either parent to exclude the father from the planning.

2. *age; health; marital status*

The fathers of the adopted children ranged in age from 18 to 53 years, with three out of five of them between 21 and 30 years old. All were believed to be in good health, but we had no reliable information about this in most instances. At least one in four of the fathers had been married, only one of them to the mother of the child. In five cases the man's marital status was not known, and in a few other situations the mother had assumed the father was single but did not really know this.

3. *education; occupation and social class*

Sometimes facts about the education of the fathers in the adopted group seemed unreliable, but there were eight who quite certainly had earned academic degrees and another nine who had diplomas of various kinds. Only five were full-time students when known to the mother, though several others were pursuing qualifications while employed in routine jobs. Table 3.6 shows the social and occupational class of the fathers of the babies, according to the Registrar General's classification.

TABLE 3.6

Social Class of 53 Natural Fathers as Determined by their Occupation

Social class	No. of fathers
I	10
II	10
III	17
IV	8
V	0
Armed services	3
Full-time students	5

4. *religion*

We do not know the religious affiliation of fathers in the overall group, but twenty-four of the adopted children were said to be Muslim, Hindu, Sikh or Buddhist with the largest number, thirteen, being Muslim. One father was Jewish, four had no religious affiliation, and in six cases the religion was unknown. Only eighteen, or one in three, were Christian, raising once again for adoption agencies the question we considered earlier regarding church affiliation as a requirement for families applying to adopt these children.

Casework with Natural Fathers

Unfortunately, there is very little done in most agencies to treat the putative father as an individual with his own needs and problems. When he is considered at all, it is likely to be only as a source of financial support or as an adjunct to the plan for the mother and child, as for example when a social and health history is needed in connection with adoption.

Many people blame the father, but few try to understand him or help him to meet his responsibilities. 'The National Council for the Unmarried Mother and Her Child thinks that little will be gained in being punitive and hostile towards fathers of children born out of wedlock, any more than towards the mothers. It does deplore, however, the fact that society tends to regard the problem as the responsibility of the mothers alone and that there is little social pressure for policies which would help fathers to feel a personal sense of responsibility and concern towards their out of wedlock children.'[7] The Child Welfare League of America, on drawing up standards for work with unmarried parents, points out that 'Wherever possible, casework rather than direct court action should be used to help the father to participate in planning and to accept financial responsibility'.[8]

The idea of working constructively with the unmarried father has not been put into practice generally either in Britain or North America. We talk and write about social work with unmarried parents, but in most agencies the work still is confined almost entirely to the mother. However, there are some notable exceptions in both countries, particularly the Church Army's work in one or two dioceses in Britain and a voluntary agency in California, both providing male caseworkers and making a special effort to offer unmarried fathers the quality of individual service heretofore recognized as essential only for the mother. The California agency believes a man caseworker provides a responsible male image with whom the fathers can form some positive identification, which will help them to face meeting their responsibility rather than avoiding it. The social worker 'takes the initiative in spelling out how this may be accomplished through standing by the girl, which lends some dignity to the relationship and is of extreme importance to her, participating in planning for the child, giving financial help, examining life problems revealed by this predicament, recognizing the means and responsibilities of fatherhood'.[9] These responsibilities would have to be interpreted somewhat differently, of course, in the case of very young fathers.

In the Project our experience in working with the fathers of the children placed for adoption was very limited, just as it was with the mothers. However, the male caseworker was able to help some fathers with their conflicting feelings about having fathered a child out of wedlock. Actually, we found that the mothers also responded well to help from a mature male social worker, perhaps seeing in him the good father figure they wished for. It appears that unmarried parents, like others in a casework situation, cast the social worker in a role consistent with their own needs and experience.

We found that a father's attitude towards his illegitimate child may be coloured by his cultural background as well as by his own emotional needs, so both must be considered. Some of the non-European fathers expected to take almost full responsibility in planning for the care of the child, others expected to share it and still others felt that this was not their concern. Some fathers felt the child should remain within his own or the mother's extended family, and these men accepted adoption only when an English mother refused to allow the baby to be sent overseas. Those fathers who did send the baby home to their family were, of course, not among the fathers in the group of adopted children. Some non-European fathers showed great affection for their child, particularly when it was their first. The baby was every bit as much theirs as though born within marriage, and they found it very hard to give him up. One father said with much feeling, 'But he is my son!' and another, 'She is my daughter, my first born.'

Concluding Remarks

All the Project's contacts with natural parents have shown individual needs and problems set against a background of cultural patterns of expected behaviour. Most girls who sought help in planning for their baby felt frightened and guilty, but beyond that each situation was highly individual and deserved to be treated as such. The situation of the English mother of a racially mixed baby was different from that of the non-European mother, but as an individual she also differed to some extent from every other English girl with a mixed race child. The Africans' problems were different from the Asians', but each girl showed her own individual response to her life experience, dependent to some extent upon her religion and social class and upon the degree to which she had become Anglicized.

In Britain's multi-racial society of today, the individual social worker cannot know as much as she would like about the cultural background of every parent who comes for help, though she can learn a good deal by listening. But she must be sure she is listening to an individual in trouble, not to a member of a group about which she has preconceived ideas and prejudices.

English mothers of racially mixed children were found to have special problems and pressures in deciding whether to try to bring up the baby or relinquish him for adoption. Grandparents often played an active part in the decision, saying in one way or another, 'If the baby were white we would keep him, but we couldn't face the neighbours with a coloured child.' Some girls were training for a career and could see no place for the child in their life. This was true of non-European mothers, too, especially those who had come to Britain at great financial sacrifice to qualify; these girls could not admit to their families back home, that they had not completed their coveted education because of sexual involvement and an unwanted pregnancy.

A girl often comes for help in making a realistic decision about the future, and when she has made the one she believes best she needs the worker's support in carrying it out. Being asked over and over whether she has made the right decision may shake her confidence, so that she retracts her decision and lets the matter drift. In that case the child's future – and her own – are determined more by default than by intent.

An unmarried mother usually faces a problem that has no really good answer. If she releases the child for adoption, she almost certainly will face a period of mourning as well as some moments of regret later on. If she cares for the child herself only out of a sense of guilt and frustration, this will present long-term difficulties. If she postpones a decision indefinitely by arranging 'temporary' care, she may feel she has failed as a mother when she finds the child never really settles anywhere, or that in settling he has made his own important relationships which do not include her. The unmarried mother may need help to see that there is no perfect solution, that some pain and regret are inherent in the situation.

If a mother is considering adoption, its finality should be made clear to her. Her ability to separate from the child can be tested in a temporary foster home, but she should not be encouraged to 'try out' adoption. There is a good deal of confusion and misunderstanding between fostering and adoption among all concerned, and this occasionally erupts in a tug of war between the natural parents and foster parents or adopters. Adoption needs to be explained with special care to West Indian and African parents, because in some countries the word denotes a relationship in which a child is brought up by a friend or relative but the natural mother can keep in touch with him and take him back later. Such an 'adoption' is more like fostering except that usually no fees are paid.

In the Project we had two mothers, both white, who reclaimed their baby girls after they had been placed for adoption. When one of these babies was placed, both the adopters and the agency were fully aware of the risk that the mother, who was receiving psychiatric treatment, might not be able to keep to a decision which she had been unable to make until the baby had had a temporary foster home and several months in a residential nursery. The mother reclaimed the child after a few days with only a temporary plan for her care.

The second mother who reclaimed did so just one week before the adoption hearing. Unwisely, the Project had offered this mother only limited service, assuming another social worker had helped her to a final decision, but actually she had moved house and had fallen between two different agency services, so no one had known the total story. When she reclaimed her baby, this mother took the child to live with her and an older illegitimate child, the only change in circumstances being better housing. If this was all that was required for the mother to keep her second child, could this not have been learned without any plans being made for adoption? Or if the mother was correct in her earlier decision that she could not give adequate care to two children as an unsupported mother, ought she not to have been helped to maintain her decision for adoption? The local authority had found a temporary foster home for the older child while the mother waited five months in a Mother and Baby Home where she cared for and grew increasingly attached to a baby she felt she could not keep. As a young woman brought up without family ties, it probably was unreasonable for us to think she would be able to maintain her decision under those conditions, and meanwhile her first child had been separated from her for over five months. This experience convinced us that an adoption agency must be sure each mother has had and continues to have adequate service and must supply it if necessary. The response of the adopters to the loss of these children will be discussed in a later chapter.

REFERENCES

(1) *Some Questions and Answers about the Work of the National Council for the Unmarried Mother and her Child*, May 1968.

(2) Fitzherbert, Katrin, *West Indian Children in London*, G. Bell & Sons, London 1967.

(3) Yelloly, Margaret A., 'The Mother's Decision', *Child Adoption*, No. 49, 1966, p. 26. Reprinted from *Sociological Review*, Vol. 13, No. 1.

(4) Meyer, Henry J., Jones, Wyatt, and Borgatta, Edger F., 'The Decision by Unmarried Mothers to Keep or Surrender Their Babies', *Social Work* (USA), Vol. 1, No. 2, April 1956, p. 108.

(5) Yelloly, *op. cit.*, p. 29.

(6) *Ibid.*, p. 30.

(7) *Some Questions and Answers about the Work of the National Council, etc.*, *op. cit.*

(8) *Child Welfare League Standards for Services to Unmarried Parents*, C.W.L.A., 1960, p. 27.

(9) Rowan, Matilde, and Pannor, Reuben, 'An Assertive Casework Approach to the Older Unmarried Father', *Child Welfare*, March 1961, p. 25.

CHAPTER 4

SELECTION OF ADOPTIVE PARENTS

Publicity to Recruit Applicants

If children are to find adoptive families there must be people willing to adopt them. The whole matter of whether or not children are considered hard to place depends on the ease with which suitable adopters can be found. Ever since the adoption of children became an acceptable middle-class way of overcoming childlessness, adoption agencies have had many more applicants than children, at least children of the kind these applicants were likely to take as sons and daughters. In many agencies this led to emphasis on finding the right child for the family rather than the other way round.

In recent years, and in some areas, the number of children needing placement increased markedly (along with the sharp rise in illegitimacy), while the number of adopters remained quite steady, thus reducing the ratio between adopters and children. At the same time, the well publicized work of people like Anna Freud, Rene Spitz, John Bowlby and Margaret Ribble caused child care agencies to be mindful of the destructive effect of uncertain living arrangements upon children, with the result that adoption has become the placement of choice for most children without other permanent ties. Such children include not only the blue-eyed baby girls from so-called 'good' families, thought to be sought after by most adoptive applicants, but older children and youngsters from all sorts of family backgrounds. Also included are some premature babies and others at risk because of physical or health handicap, and children of mixed or non-white parentage. For all these children there has never been a waiting list of adopters, so agencies concerned with the needs of these children have had to take some action to recruit applicants. Even in 1968 and 1969, when the total number of children needing adoption fell markedly and resulted in a surplus of would-be adopters, special efforts were required to attract applicants for the child who was 'different'.

When the Project was set up to place fifty non-white babies, it was expected that the task of encouraging people to apply to the Project would be a major undertaking. Actually this task proved simpler than had been expected and enough suitable applicants were quite easily recruited. The university setting and the emphasis on research have been offered as explanations, but these factors could just as easily have frightened away some other applicants. Certainly the interest and splendid co-operation of the press were factors; so were the interest and alertness of children's departments and other agencies in referring hopeful applicants.

When the Project began in April 1965, it inherited seventy-six applications and a larger number of inquiries from an earlier ISS project which had brought children from Hong Kong to Britain for adoption. Many of these applications and inquiries were of long standing. Some of the families lived outside the Project's area of operation which had been set at fifty miles around London; others only wanted a child from Hong Kong or were no longer wishing to adopt any child. Those who were interested in a non-white child born in Britain, but who lived too far from London, were referred to their local authority or other adoption societies in their area. We do not know how many of these went on to adopt a non-white child.

While the applicants remaining from the Hong Kong Project were being sorted out, the staff also made contact with many social agencies and medical officers of health in and around London to seek their co-operation in making the Project known. A simple three-page leaflet was prepared by the staff and committee, explaining the Project in a few words and pictures. This was enclosed in the reply to every inquiry and was distributed in bulk to local children's officers, medical officers of health, infant welfare clinics, public libraries, moral welfare workers and some religious groups.

Weekly newspapers in the Home Counties were approached and many ran editorials about the Project and the need for adopters. The national press picked this up and both the *Guardian* and *The Times* published small articles about the Project which brought in about fifty inquiries, nearly all from middle-class people, many from outside the Project area. Six applicants within the Project area went on to adopt a child through the Project. Then the *Daily Mirror* became interested and in December 1965 backed the Project with a very effective half-page feature article. This resulted in nearly four hundred inquiries from all over the country, some being clearly unsuitable. Those who lived outside the Project area were immediately advised to apply to their local authority or some other adoption agency in their area, but again we do not know how many did so. Those in the Project area were considered along with other inquiries as quickly as possible. Some people who had read the story wrote in as long as two years later. Seven children were placed with applicants who first learned of the Project from the *Daily Mirror* story, including two couples who had come to England from the Caribbean and several English families, mostly upper working class or artisans. Later, the *Sunday Mirror* and the *Evening Standard* printed articles which resulted in a total of three placements.

The *Daily Mirror* article caught the interest of several weekly journals which published stories in 1966, and at the same time various church magazines as well as *Midwives Chronicle, Maternal and Child Care Journal* and several women's magazines mentioned the Project. Four of our adoptive families said they first learned of the Project in this way. In 1967 and 1968 the staff and committee decided against a radio or television appeal since a small but steady number of inquiries continued to come in and produced enough adopters for the Project to exceed its goal of fifty placements.

The difficulty with the use of the mass media in home-finding is that it reaches the general public rather than any particular segment of it that might be expected to respond usefully to the message. This results in a deluge of inquiries and relatively few placements. People are apt to act impulsively on learning of needy children, and then have second thoughts when talking it over with husband or wife and considering adoption within the reality of their lives. This kind of publicity also needs to be considered in relation to staff time, as we cannot seek help from the public and then take our time about following up their inquiries. Generalized publicity is likely to mean dropping everything else, so that a large number of not very hopeful replies can be sorted out. A more focused appeal is likely to result in fewer but more useful replies. However, so little was known about the placement of non-white children in Britain at the time the Project was seeking adopters that no one knew where or on whom to focus the appeal. For example, it was expected that all or most of the applicants would be English couples living in the home counties who might be reached through the national or local press. Whether they would be childless couples or families likely to read parents' magazines was not known. Whether they would be weekly wage-earners, business people or professionals was no more than a guess, or we might have tried the more specialized publications. If we were launching the appeal again we should seek some publicity in journals published by West Indians, Asians and Africans in Britain with the hope of interesting more applicants from among these people. Our experience leads us to believe that any general publicity should stress that many of the children needing homes are Anglo-West Indian. Much of our publicity reached people only wanting an Asian or Anglo-Asian child.

As the Project came to an end, inquiries continued to come in at the rate of about eight a month, and we were able to refer these people to the most appropriate member agency in the Adoption Resource Exchange, certain that the requests would be followed up. Since the Project has been completed, the Adoption Resource Exchange acts as a centre for all inquiries and sees that they are followed up by member agencies. If the inquiry becomes an application, it is studied by an agency that works co-operatively with other members in the Exchange to bring together suitable applicants and children, even if they live in different parts of the country.

Pre-application Group Meetings

The pre-application group meeting is a well established method in a great many adoption agencies in North America and although it is now used increasingly in Britain, we think the Project may have been the first British agency to use it. The staff had confidence in this method and decided to make regular use of it. The purpose was to:

1. Tell people who wished to adopt through the Project a little of what this would involve for them in terms of the Project's methods, the kinds of babies needing homes and the adopters' involvement in the research.

2. Give those who were ambivalent, or who could see that they were not eligible or who did not wish to take part in the research, a chance to withdraw easily without filing an application or having a personal interview.

3. Start people thinking about some of the things we would want to discuss with them in interviews, so they would be better informed and less anxious about what to expect.

The content of the pre-application group meetings was factual, but we said that in interviews we should want to discuss feelings and motives. Members of the group were not asked to answer any questions in the meeting, but they had plenty of opportunities to put questions to the staff. Some of the same questions arose at almost every meeting: 'How long will it take to be approved?', 'How long after we are approved before we can get a child?', 'Will the baby's mother be able to take him away before we go to court?', 'Will we have any choice about the child we get?' In the material presented by the staff member it was important to give only the most relevant information, and to avoid a heavy emphasis on problems, as we were screening applicants in, not out, to meet the needs of a variety of children. We tried to give a definite idea of how long it would be before the first interview could be arranged, as we knew this would help to allay anxiety and avoid hostility towards the Project because of any waiting period. We mentioned that medical examinations and references would be required, and that the local children's department, health department and the police would be contacted as required by regulation. It was felt that too many facts and figures would confuse people, as it is known they can take away only what has meaning for them. They did seem to gain some understanding of agency policies, and usually agreed that the Project could not be expected to look for children for adopters, but only for homes for the children to whom it owed its first responsibility. Workers in other agencies have made this same observation,[1] and some of the Project adopters later told us they decided to extend their interest to a wider range of children as a result of the meeting.

Meeting the staff and learning something about the agency at first hand seemed to reduce anxiety, so that those who decided to make an application were ready to participate quite freely in the first interview. In the group meeting nothing had been asked of them, but they had been given information freely and there had been a chance to take the measure of the staff and their fellow applicants. There was often a marked relaxation by the end of the meeting, and usually one or two couples lingered afterwards to ask another question or tell of someone's experience of adoption.

A meeting of six or eight couples and social workers around a large table or in a circle gave everyone a chance to see everyone else and usually encouraged participation. Meetings were held in the evening or at weekends to ensure attendance of husbands. Tea or coffee helped people to feel welcome and free to talk with one another and with the staff.

The real give and take of group discussion was not often found in these meetings, as applicants were unsure what opinions would be acceptable. Neither did one usually find leadership developing within the group since this was the one and only time all these people were to meet together. One might have expected to see group process here if the meeting had been the first of several to be held as part of the family study and preparation for adoptive parenthood, but in the Project we did not make use of groups for this purpose.

Aside from the benefits accruing to members of the group, the staff was able to give information about the agency and adoption to several couples in much the same time it would have taken to explain this to one couple. This freed the time of the first interview for its real purpose, which was consideration of the couple's wish to adopt and their suitability to perform in that role. When a social worker feels very unsure of herself in adoption, she may not welcome this method and may prefer to use the first interview to give information about the agency, since that is a safe subject and one she feels adequate to handle.

At the Project meetings, application forms were made available to be taken home by those who wanted them. Others, who by now realized they were clearly ineligible, or who were uncertain or only at the stage of exploring adoption as a possibility for some remote future, were spared the need for a personal interview and rejection, and staff time was released for work with those who did send in an application. There is question about how much significance should be given to a couple's behaviour in a meeting, as a person's ability to perform well in a group may have little or nothing to do with his performance in the quite different role of a parent. One does occasionally see inter- action between husband and wife, which gives some clue to the quality of their relationship and the mutuality of their interest in adoption. As for the couples' feelings about the staff, the meeting should leave them confident the agency knows what it is doing, and that applica- tions will be dealt with fairly and in relation to the number and needs of the children to be placed. Obviously, staff members involved in the meeting should have a good knowledge of agency policies and the kinds of children likely to be needing families.

The Project held twenty-five pre-application group meetings in three years and altered its methods somewhat in the light of experience. We said a bit more about the children likely to be available, because we found people often had quite mistaken ideas about what these children of different racial backgrounds would be like, while non-white applicants wanted to know if there might be children of their own racial background.

Two hundred and fifty couples were invited to the 25 meetings and 179 attended. Of these, 122 were later interviewed and 49 eventually went on to adopt a child. (Only four applications were studied without attendance first at a group meeting; two of them later took a child.) As can be seen, the average number of couples invited to a meeting was ten and the average attendance was seven couples. The average number interviewed from each meeting was five couples of whom an average of two per meeting went on to adopt a baby through the Project. We do not know how this ratio of successful applicants and the number attending the pre-application group meetings compares with the experience of other agencies or whether, in fact, any other agency has held such meetings exclusively for people considering the adoption of a non-white child. The meetings did make it possible to give attention to a large number of inquiries with a small staff, and resulted in a workable number of actual applications in relation to the number of children the Project expected to place.

The First Interview

The Project staff felt this was the most important interview and should take place in the agency office with husband and wife together after an application had been made. Making and keeping an appointment that involves some action on the part of the applicants is one test of interest and readiness. This is harder to gauge if we go to them. Normally this interview can be scheduled during regular office hours, but we found that some husbands could not be absent from work without jeopardizing their employment. This was most often true of men in skilled or semi-skilled occupations, especially immigrants, but some husbands worked on shifts or were finished in the late afternoon.

The Project tried to arrange for one caseworker to carry through with the adopters from the first interview to the end of the Project, but staff changes made this impossible in some cases. If an agency has very limited professional staff and little confidence in its interviewers it may expect to use more than one worker to consider each application. Where this is the situation, the first interview is the place for the most skilled worker. It is important to have a prompt assessment at this stage of the application by someone able to make a decision and given authority to do this, so that the hopeful applications can be accepted for study, and the unhopeful helped to withdraw.

When an application cannot be accepted, it can be done with less harm to the applicants and the agency if it is done early before people have become deeply involved with the agency. Some case committees expect to make this decision, in which case the worker can only advise the applicants that she believes the committee is unlikely to accept the application and she will notify them when the committee has met. Some committees will not accept a staff recommendation for rejection after only one interview and insist upon the study being completed, including medical reports and references. This subjects applicants to unnecessary procedures, wastes staff time and turns the caseworker into little more than a gatherer of information. A committee employing professional staff will do well to consider the worker's recommendation not to proceed further with a family study when it has become clear that the agency cannot place a child in this family. The Adoption Act, 1958, requires a committee to approve all placements. It does not require committee approval to decide that an applicant will not make a good adopter. Committees may rightly wish to know the reasons why applications are being turned down and make some general policies about criteria for accepting or rejecting them, so that staff members will know what is expected of them. Like most other people, social workers are likely to be more responsible and careful when they know the responsibility is theirs and cannot be passed along to others.

The first interview offers the best chance to hear what the applicants feel it is important to tell us, and we do well to listen. They may tell us things we should never have thought to ask, but which are going to be important in this instance. If the application form is a good one, it has given us most of the factual information we need and has been signed by both husband and wife, so there is no reason to go over all this again or to get into a question and answer sesssion that discourages applicants from discussing their feelings and attitudes.

As time goes on, social workers are less sure they know exactly what adoptive parents need to be like in order to perform well in that role, and they are looking to follow-up studies for guidance in this. Although people with potentially good prospects usually can be distinguished from those who are very poor risks, there is much less certainty about the others. The combination of factors is different in each instance and each application has to be considered on its own merits with the assets and liabilities weighed and without the expectation of perfection. Certainly 'nice people' and financial security are no longer the important factors in selecting adopters.

E

As Dr Viola Bernard an American psychiatrist with many years' experience as consultant to adoption agencies, has said, 'We seek couples who are on good adult terms with themselves and with each other, who are ready for adoption psychologically and situationally, and whose desire for children stems from emotionally healthy needs and capacities'.[2] This is purposely general and open to individual interpretation, but the key words are probably 'adult', 'ready' and 'healthy', of which 'ready' is the most difficult to assess and perhaps the most important. Fortunately, if we are prepared to offer some casework service, we may be able to help some applicants become more ready to accept their role as adopters and to cherish a child not born to them. We can explore with them whether adoption will be a satisfactory solution for the needs and desires that brought them to the agency, and whether they can meet the needs of the kinds of children the agency is seeking to place for adoption. We can help them think through their reasons for wanting to adopt and recognize with them that there is likely to be more than one reason, some obvious and others much less so.

In interviewing applicants seeking to adopt a child across ethnic lines, we felt that the basic motivation should be desire to increase the size of the family, to have a child or an additional child, as in any adoption application. Other factors such as concern about over-population, racial integration, and the plight of homeless children – a sort of room for one more attitude – often entered into the application and we felt these were very acceptable reasons, provided they were firmly based on the wish to bring up a child as an individual in his own right and as a full member of the family. Most of the couples who applied to the Project were people concerned about social problems and anxious to do their bit, but those who went on to adopt a baby were those who most of all wanted a larger family and chose this way to combine their needs and interests. Workers need to be careful that they do not let their own feelings about interracial adoption cast suspicion upon the motivation of others. This is particularly pertinent to workers who have had little experience in placing children across racial lines and find it hard to believe that someone might wish such an adoption for perfectly healthy reasons.

Workers are so accustomed to thinking applicants are seeking a child like one they might have borne, that they sometimes forget how important it is for adoptive parents to be able to accept that the child is not their biological child and that there is a difference between adopting and having a child naturally. Applicants to adopt a child of different race are more often ready to accept this difference. Many of them already have natural-born children and do not need to be concerned about infertility or the wish to have a child that resembles them. This wish has been fulfilled in their biological children and they can accept and love a child very different from themselves in appearance and possibly different in other ways as well. Childless couples seeking to adopt a child of different race are in a different position, and most of those in the Project wanted a light child whom they could see as in some way resembling them in appearance, even though to other people the difference might be more apparent than the resemblance. There were exceptions to this, as we also had two such couples who were very happy with a really brown-skinned child.

Subsequent Interviews
In the Project no set number of interviews was planned, because some people were easier to know than others or came to the agency more nearly ready to make a full commitment to a child's future. Case-workers tried to involve couples in a kind of self-study about their reasons for wishing to take this step and about the satisfactions and problems they could foresee in it. Sometimes this was accomplished in three or four interviews, but usually more were required or the interviews were spread over a somewhat longer period to give time for applicants to think things through and explore their feelings before discussing them further with the worker.

The first interview should have given the worker clues to be followed up in later interviews. At least one of these interviews must be in the home, as required by law, but the others can be in the home or office. If there are young children it may be difficult for the wife to come to the office several times, but often it is more satisfactory to interview the husband alone at the office if at all possible. It is exceedingly difficult to have a good home interview with husband or wife alone if the other is in the house, particularly if it is a small house or flat. It is important to know each as an individual, but also to assess them as a couple able to communicate meaningfully with each other about things that are important to either of them.

If the couple is childless or unable to have another child, feelings of each partner about this need to be brought out. This is true also of a recent miscarriage or the death of a child in the family. An adopted child cannot be expected to replace another child and must be wanted for himself, which is unlikely if parents have sought to adopt before they have faced their loss and expressed their grief. Some discussion about illegitimacy and the problems of unmarried parents must be included, since adopters will need to come to an acceptance of an adopted child's background in order to handle this with him later on in a helpful way. Of course, this is part of their ability to accept and live with difference, and to see parenthood as a commitment to being mother and father to a child who is a growing individual in his own right. Most of this is equally appropriate for families who can have natural born children, except that here one does not have to deal with feelings about infertility and childlessness.

In working with applicants to adopt a child of mixed race, we accepted that prejudice of one kind or another may be present in everyone. It would seem important for interracial adopters, though, to have no more than a minimal amount of mild prejudice in any area, not only regarding race and colour but in relation to illegitimacy, unwed parents, religion or any of the people or things that so often call up intense feelings of intolerance. Like all adopters they must be able to accept difference, only more of it. We also felt the outcome of an adoption might be more hopeful if the adopters were able to think and act independently, not as isolated personalities, but as people with a positive outlook on life and the future, with more concern for people than for what people think of them.

It may be as important for the social worker to understand her own prejudices as it is to understand those of the applicants. Certainly, she needs to examine her own feelings about interracial adoption before she can hope to assess these feelings in her applicants. Does she really think a white family is unwise to adopt a coloured child? Does she think it is unfair to the other children in the family or that the parents will not be able to treat a mixed family of white and coloured children equally? Does she distrust the motives of these families and fear they will not treat the adopted child well? We have learned of agencies which are so sceptical of a white family's motives in seeking a coloured child that they feel it necessary always to place two such children in the same family, presumably so one will not be 'odd man out'. However, everyone who wants to adopt one child does not want or feel able to care for two, and there is no assurance that two adopted children will like each other better than they like other members of the family. It would seem that one of the adopted children could feel very much left out if the other adopted child happened to prefer a natural-born child in the family. Surely, we are looking for families who will be sensitive to the needs of individual children and who will accept the adopted child, of whatever race, as a complete member of the family, but we shall not be able to distinguish which families can do this until we have come to terms with some of our own feelings about race and perhaps also about adoption.

Children in the Family

Children already in the family, whether natural born or adopted, as well as children the family plan for later, need to be taken into consideration. Perhaps this is even more important when the adopted child is to be of different race. Many applicants understandably felt this would be an enriching experience for the whole family and found it hard to foresee problems arising from the presence of a dark-skinned child in the family. We felt they were ready in this respect, when they could accept the possibility of problems for themselves and for their other children, as well as for the adopted child, but were prepared to meet these as a family without being overwhelmed by them.

Workers tried to plan for the adopted baby to enter the family when the other children were prepared for his arrival and seemed able to accept him, rather than at a time when a child in the family was going through a difficult period, such as starting school or nursery school or convalescing from an illness. We did not go along with requests to bring up a child of the same age or older than a child already in the home, and we felt it important to have a reasonable difference in age between the youngest biological child and the adopted child. Experience in the Project suggested that for an adopted child to be less than a year younger than the youngest biological child was not always in the best interest of either of these, but could cause difficulties, especially for the child already in the home. On the other hand, considerably older children often helped the new child to settle into the family.

The Project workers made a real effort to get to know a family's natural-born children and to learn how they felt about the plans for an adopted brother or sister. They believed children were entitled to their point of view and should have a chance to express it. Sometimes it was possible to have a brief talk alone with an older child, but they were also seen with their parents because only in this way could one assess the quality of the relationship between parents and their children. Mealtimes and the children's bedtime, of course, are ideal times for seeing how parents handle their children. One also can learn how much these people enjoy their children, whereas the unpredictability of this is one of the hazards of assessing applicants who have not yet had the experience of parenthood. These applicants also know what is involved in the care of children and what they can expect in taking on another youngster.

Medical Assessment

When a child receives a new family by adoption, it is hoped that the adopters will live in reasonably good health until he grows up. Life expectancy is always uncertain if only because of the frequency of accidental deaths, but the applicants' past and present health often indicates something about future illness and longevity.

This is clearly outside the social worker's field of competence and is a matter for the medical profession. The Project followed the practice of most adoption agencies and required a full and up-to-date medical examination of each of the applicants by their own general practitioner. Forms for these reports were worked out by staff and medical consultant,[3] and a copy was sent to the applicants' family doctor with a covering letter explaining the nature of the Project and the reason the report was requested. The Association of British Adoption Agencies now provides very detailed and comprehensive forms for reporting health history and medical examinations for both children and adopters, but these were not available in time for the Project.

Early in the Project only the social work staff reviewed the medical reports in cases where the family doctor recommended the applicants. Only if a report contained something worrying or unclear, did the worker discuss it with the family's doctor or with one of the Project's medical consultants, who then interpreted the findings or sought additional tests or reports. However, the social workers found they did not always agree on what was worrying. This convinced them that they were not qualified to interpret medical findings, so it was arranged for the medical consultant to review all medical reports, and this proved very much more satisfactory. The Project also was fortunate in having a psychiatric consultant to evaluate reports of past mental or emotional illness or a physical condition likely to have serious emotional implications. Obviously, the social worker still needed to know what was on the form and its significance, since it was she who was working with the family, but it was the medical and psychiatric consultants who could interpret the significance of the medical findings in terms of foreseeable illness, handicap or life expectancy.[4]

Some agencies like to start by obtaining the medical reports, so it will not be necessary to interview applicants who may be disqualified for medical reasons. This is understandable from an administrative point of view in a busy agency, but it may give the impression that the medical aspects are the most important. Under this procedure, applicants rejected for medical reasons have not even had a chance to discuss their reasons for coming to the agency or their feelings about it. In the Project, health was always discussed in the first interview and, if a problem existed, the applicants were asked to have the medical examinations as the next step, but in all other cases medical examinations were done later, after the worker knew the family well. This meant that the need for examinations, and the accompanying expense to the family, were required only for those applicants who were most likely to be accepted. Only six applications were withdrawn or rejected on the advice of their doctor because of serious health conditions.

Interviews with Significant Relatives
It has not been a usual feature of adoption practice to discuss the proposed adoption with the applicants' parents or other relatives, but the Project staff felt that this might be wise when a couple wished to adopt a child of different race. This has proved rewarding, though one or two adopters later told us they had found this procedure difficult to accept.

At the pre-application group meeting, those present were urged to share their adoption plans with their parents or other close relatives, because real opposition from them might make the plan unworkable or at least much more difficult. Visits to relatives were usually made after several interviews with the applicants themselves. They were always by appointment and with the knowledge of the applicants. There were prospective grandparents who completely accepted the adoption plan and were looking forward to the new grandchild, but there were others who were lukewarm about the idea, as well as some who opposed it. A few felt their children did not realize what they were doing, and several were concerned for the effect on the other children in the family. Some found it hard to accept the idea of adoption when a couple could have more children born to them, or when they already had three or four children. Most felt the decision was one for the applicants to make, and they would accept the decision even though they did not consider it a good idea. Most were glad to have been involved even if they could not endorse the plan wholeheartedly, and in some cases it seemed to help to talk it out and to inquire about the caseworker's experience with other families. People in this age group are rather inclined to avoid taking unnecessary risks, and it is not strange that they should be more reluctant than their children to try something as new as adopting a non-white child into a family of natural-born white children. Rather, it is interesting that so many were enthusiastic about the adoption, or at least were willing to go along with it and welcome the adopted child into the extended family on a par with the other grandchildren, giving him what a Glasgow child psychiatrist recently called 'the adopted child's only link with ancestry'.[5]

The Use of References

Adoption applicants are asked to name two or three persons to whom the agency can refer for information about them. They are expected to give people who have known them intimately, preferably for a good many years, rather than community leaders who can only vouch for their reputation in the community. As social workers have become better trained and more skilful in evaluating people, there is much less dependence upon references. Often the caseworker comes to know the family more intimately than the referees do, but she is still glad to have another opinion if only to confirm her own impression. The responsibility rests with her, though, and not with the applicants' friends, who are just that and very likely to see them in the most favourable light.

In the Project we interviewed referees unless the applicants had come to the area very recently and all their friends were in another part of the country. In such a case an individual letter was sent. A form letter or questionnaire is likely to be ineffective in contributing anything to the agency's understanding of the applicants as potential adoptive parents. We did find that referees more often than relatives genuinely supported the applicants' plan to adopt a child. Occasionally, referees can be a real help in understanding applicants, but more often the result is to lull the social worker into believing only the best about a family, while ignoring her own doubts and uncertainties.

Handling Rejected Applications

Some time ago, when agencies had several times as many applicants as children they considered suitable for adoption, it was customary to set rather rigid age limits and various other arbitrary requirements which automatically screened out some of the excess applications. Those who passed these requirements, but were eliminated after study of their application, usually were told that it was possible to place a baby with only about one in ten applicants and they had not been chosen. This was understandable and probably not too hurtful in most instances, but neither was it very helpful. Some other agencies did – and still do – end the matter by writing the briefest of letters saying the application has not been accepted by the agency's committee, but giving no reason. This may save the agency a good deal of work and the need to justify its decisions, but it leaves the applicants in the unenviable position of having shared their innermost thoughts and feelings, only to have them rejected without knowing what was wrong. Certainly there are situations in which knowledge of the reasons could be harmful to the applicants, but there are many more in which the thinking of the staff or committee is so woolly as to make a reasonable explanation impossible.

This is not to say that handling rejected applications is easy. It probably is one of the most difficult tasks in casework and few will agree upon how it should be done, but there are a few principles to serve as guidelines. The applicants should know that the decision must rest with the agency, since it has responsibility for the children who are to be placed, but that the worker appreciates the sense of failure and frustration that this rejection brings to the applicants. It needs to be remembered that adoptive applicants are very vulnerable at this time, especially those who have not been able to have biological children and are now being denied adoptive parenthood as well. To have their application rejected often confirms their own doubts about their ability to be good parents and is all the more painful because of this. The best service the agency can give to adoptive parents who must be refused is to help them withdraw their request, thus avoiding altogether the traumatic implications of refusal.[6] When they do not withdraw, the worker can at least be sensitive to the applicants' pain and avoid increasing it. She can be aware of the great importance the decision holds for the couple, and can convey her respect and confidence in them as persons, even when she does not feel confident of them in the specialized role of adopters. If it is kept in mind that it is the application and not the applicants themselves that cannot be approved, the agency is then entirely free to accept the applicants as people.

In the Project we tried to follow these principles, though in one or two instances we were unable to help disappointed applicants to accept our decision. The scarcity of adoptive parents for non-white children and the element of goodwill and generosity involved in some applications from families with natural-born children made rejection of applications even harder to understand. Most people felt they certainly could offer a child much more than a Children's Home or a foster home, but the Project took the view that a marginal home was not good enough, that the problems inherent in adopting a child of different race called for the very best. Mistakes may have been made in assessing the best and the marginal, but the intention was to select those most able to accept the child's individuality and background and to assimilate him into their family.

Preparation for Adoptive Parenthood

Some of the research in North America and in Britain has made social workers less sure of their ability to predict which applicants will make good adoptive parents. Many workers now feel more able to spot the major indicators of future difficulties, than to predict characteristics that will result in good adoptive parenting. At the same time, differences in natural and adoptive parenthood have become clearer. There is increased acceptance of David Kirk's idea that people come to adoption unprepared for their role, which is different from natural parenthood, and need help in accepting and coping with this role.[7] Dr Kirk and a very few others, particularly in North America, see the agency's work as education of applicants to fulfil their role, instead of assessment of the life history and personality structure of the applicants.

In the Project we did not feel ready to discard the assessment of applicants in favour of their education, but we did feel that applicants adopting a child of different race from themselves would be particularly vulnerable to what Dr Kirk calls 'role handicap' and would need help with this. There would be no models or accepted ways to follow in moving into interracial adoptive parenthood and these adopters might encounter the most inappropriate expectations and responses from family, friends and community. So the Project workers tried to develop the applicants' potentialities for interracial adoptive parenthood and considered this an important part of the family study. Very often, the period between approval of the application and the placement of a child with the family was used to continue this preparation, and the post-adoption discussion groups for adoptive parents took this one step further. The same material was covered a number of times with slightly different focus, as experience of the adopters in their new role gave new meaning to such subjects as the responses of other people, telling the child about adoption and about his background, and bringing up a racially mixed family of natural-born and adopted children. As staff members gained experience in interracial adoption they were able to be more helpful in preparing adopters, but they soon found that the need for this was not confined to those adopting across ethnic lines. Experience with applicants of other races, who sought a child of their own racial background, confirmed that these adopters, too, knew little of what adoption would involve for them and welcomed help in taking on this new role. It seems to us that the adoption agency has a dual function with adoptive applicants – assessment and preparation.

Second Child Applications

The Project did not share the view of some agency workers and committees who believe people who adopt one child should be urged to adopt a second a year or two later. This seemed to us a highly individual matter. When our adopters mentioned the possibility of another child we were rather non-committal, leaving it entirely to them to decide if and when they would make a second application. Many of the Project adopters already had children born to them and some planned to have more, but even where the adopted baby was the only child we felt this was not necessarily bad. The evidence from various pieces of follow up research on the effect of the presence of other children in the family, whether natural-born or adopted, is quite inconclusive, and the research done by Glatzer in 1955 and Lye in 1958 shows no support for the popular belief that 'only' children are problem children.[8]

Experience has shown that adoptive parents are inclined to be more particular about the second child and more anxious about his background, perhaps because their need for a child is less great now that they have one, but also because they are now building their family around the first child and want any others to fit in well with him. An example of this was seen when Project adopters willing to take a first child of any race, preferred a second child of the same combination of races and with the same general appearance and degree of colour as the first. Although several families mentioned another child, only two actually made an application and had a second child placed with them before the end of the Project. A revised application form brought the factual information on these families up to date, and interviews with them were focused largely on the present and future. We wanted to be sure there was room in the applicants' lives for another adopted child, that he would be loved for himself and was not sought primarily as a companion for the first, or to avoid bringing up an only child or one child of different race in a family of white children. There was discussion in preparation for handling the jealousy of the older child in his need to share his parents with a younger brother or sister. In at least one family that decided not to apply for a second child, the first was so entirely satisfactory that any other would always be second best.

A study made in 1967 by the Standing Conference of Societies Registered for Adoption found that more than three out of five of the children returned to voluntary agencies without being adopted were second child placements. This makes it all too clear that placing a second child in a family we already know is not just an easy way of getting another child placed, but calls for real understanding of the factors involved in each situation.

Applicants of other Races and Cultures
Some agencies feel they do not know how to assess people of other races and cultures. They are uncertain what these people expect in a child and how well they will take care of a youngster. Others simply say, 'We treat all our applicants the same'.

There are some differences here and they need to be explored. While casework with people of other races and cultures involves the same concern for the individual and his problem that is the basis of any good casework, it needs to be applied here with special sensitivity. This sensitivity includes awareness of the unfortunate barriers that exist between races in today's world. The barrier is by no means insurmountable, but social workers do need to be aware of the role played by their own and the applicants' feelings about racial and cultural difference.

An adoption application is a threatening experience in almost any circumstances, especially for childless couples, but we can expect the experience to be particularly so for applicants who are being interviewed by a worker of different race.[9] This is a situation that may recall all the couple's past experience with white people in positions of authority. The attitude towards the worker may be affected by an experience of discrimination in housing or employment, causing the applicants to wonder if this person too will treat them as second-class citizens. They may wonder if she will understand their ways or if she will be critical of them. Can she understand their striving to improve their social and economic status and perhaps to become more completely English? It is likely to be very hard for them to discuss with a white worker their inability to have a child of their own, and if theirs is a racially mixed marriage they may wonder how the worker will accept this.

How *does* the worker feel about mixed marriages? In fact, how does she feel about people who look very different from herself and sometimes are of a very different religious and cultural background? If she has been brought up on the symbolism of light and dark, as representing good and evil, it may be easier for her to believe some of the mythology she has heard about black people, or the applicants' racial group in particular, than to see the promise this couple holds as parents to an adopted child.

What makes this all so difficult is that social workers usually view racial bias as unacceptable, and this leads them to deny or suppress whatever negative attitudes they may have. They honestly believe they have no prejudice, but at the same time some of them go on evaluating individuals on the basis of stereotyped ideas about people of that race, religion or nationality. The Chinese are inscrutable; Indians are mystics; West Indians are cheerful and happy-go-lucky: these are the kinds of generalizations usually learned early in life, and that make it hard to see the individual as he really is. As social workers, we must examine our feelings and prejudices or they will stand like a wall between us and our non-white applicants. As social workers we need to see beyond our own white middle-class values and learn to appreciate people whose life style is different from our own, but who may be able to accept and love an adopted child.

We cannot know much about the wide variety of cultures found in Britain today, but we can listen and learn. One of the things that agencies may find frustrating is that everyone's sense of time is not the same as ours. Not all people are ruled by the clock, as we are. In some cultures people are very casual about time and may arrive early or late for appointments, sometimes not even on the right day. With these people, this should not be interpreted as lack of interest without looking further into the matter. Different customs in the use of names and in designating family relationships can cause misunderstanding between agencies and adoptive applicants. For example, some Muslim wives do not take their husband's name, but others do; it depends upon the custom in the family. Muslim names may include a Muslim title in addition to the personal names by which the person is known. Sometimes there is no family name at all, so all members of the family may have entirely different names. Sikh names include the title Singh for men and Kaur for women, placed between the personal and family names. Hindu names simply have one or more personal names followed by the subcaste name which is the surname for the family.[10] We have found that people from the Caribbean area may be known by two or more completely different names, with the result that birth records, marriage certificates and passport names may not all be the same. This is confusing for the social worker, but should not be allowed to interfere with adoption, as it has nothing to do with the quality of the parenting these people can give to an adopted child. The same holds for the confusion caused by the custom of speaking of aunts, uncles and cousins as mother, father, brother or sister. This arises from an extended family system in which these relationships are largely socially synonymous.

The social worker may be surprised to find that her West Indian applicants lived together before their marriage. This is the usual and accepted practice among working-class people on some of the islands of the West Indies. They look forward to marriage as soon as their economic condition will permit a proper wedding, but this may take many years. If the applicants have maintained a stable relationship and are now married, it should be possible to consider them as adopters. The matter of working mothers also arises in considering West Indian couples, since it is customary for a West Indian woman to support or help support the children by working outside the home, while her mother looks after the children. In coming to Britain, West Indians hope to improve their socio-economic status, and in most cases this can be done only if both husband and wife are employed. The wife usually expects to work and her husband expects her to do so. This poses a problem for adoption agencies unaccustomed to placing children with working mothers. But without this joint income, most West Indians in Britain would have little hope of adequate housing and of achieving the standard of living usually expected of adoptive parents.

In the Project, we began by refusing applicants if the woman insisted on continuing to work outside the home, but we became more flexible as time went on, considering each case on its merits. It was important, as always, to be sure the mother really wanted to be a mother, and that she had enough energy for both jobs so that she could enjoy whatever free time she had with her child. We wanted to be sure she planned to work because it was necessary in the marriage, and not because she saw her responsibility to care for her children as of secondary importance. Another important question was what provision the adopters could make for the child's care during the mother's working hours when a willing grandmother was not available. We placed a baby with a mother who planned to return to work after three months maternity leave, but we felt confident of the deep desire of these applicants to be good parents, and they had already brought up a relative's child quite successfully, while getting settled in Britain and working hard to buy a comfortable home. Our experience with this family to the end of the Project more than justified the risks. The baby was well loved and was daily-minded by a devoted next-door neighbour, while the adoptive mother had found employment nearer home so she could spend more time with the child. Another West Indian adoptive mother returned to work when the baby was somewhat older, but a grandmother living with the family cared for the child during the mother's working hours. Even the Child Welfare League of America has taken a more realistic attitude toward working mothers, and in its revision of its *Standards for Adoption Practice*[11] the League now says, 'A woman who works should not for that reason alone be excluded from consideration as an adoptive applicant if she is able to remain at home with the child for as long as necessary after placement (the length of time will depend on the child's age and previous experiences) and to provide security for the child by continuity of relationships and of responsible care.' A recent American follow-up study found that one in five adoptive mothers in the study were employed.[12]

The matter of housing is a problem for people of other races who have come to Britain. This is no less so for people who want to adopt a child than it is for others, so some flexibility is called for on the part of social workers and their committees. However, most of the twenty-three non-white applicants to the Project were buying a house, so it may be that newcomers to Britain are not very likely to seek to adopt a child until they are well settled here and have a comfortable home.

We cannot expect that people from other parts of the world will necessarily be Christian, or that the Christian sect they belong to will necessarily be recognized by the British churches. However, as reported in Chapter 3, the natural mothers or fathers of many non-European children in Britain are adherents of other faiths, or of none, and are not very much interested in the religion of the adopters, as long as they will offer their child warmth and acceptance. Are applicants being rejected because they do not meet the religious requirements of the agencies?

We have heard some adoption workers say they would not place a little girl with Muslim adopters because they feel the Muslim attitude towards women would interfere with the child's development as an individual. But with Muslim girls needing homes is it right to judge the Muslim culture by our own set of values? Probably Muslims who are adhering strictly to Muslim custom would seek a boy. However, as people become more Anglicized they are likely to mix English customs with their own ways, and one finds some of the strict customs being dropped, particularly among well-educated business and professional families. In most of the mixed marriages that have come to our attention, the English wife had the same status as any other English wife; she did not assume the subservient attitude of an Asian woman. This is a time of change that requires us to be alert to the way each couple is adjusting to life in Britain.

Non-white applicants often feel that white social workers will not understand the things that are important to them in a child's appearance. No wonder, when Negro couples are known to have been offered an Asian child! That the child is coloured is not enough. Rivalries and ancient feuds exist among the various darker-skinned races, just as they do between the white and coloured races. Most adopters hope for a child of racial background like their own and many have feelings about depth of colour, facial features, body build and especially the type of hair. For a Negro girl long hair is especially valued and it should not be cut while in temporary care. Many people prefer a child somewhat lighter than themselves because of the value placed on a light skin and the accompanying advantages to the child in a society dominated by white people. In some groups, degree of colour is also tied in with social class, with the result that it is unusual for a couple to seek a child darker or more Negroid or Asian in appearance than themselves. On the other hand, in our experience very dark-skinned Africans or West Indians sometimes sought a very dark-skinned child with truly Negroid features and hair. One must learn each couple's expectations, and then not be too surprised if they still do not take the first child offered because they do not feel drawn to a child of his appearance. However, it is an unpleasant experience to reject a child, so we do not want to subject a couple to this when it can be avoided.

A study was made in Pittsburgh, Pennsylvania, in 1956,[13] to learn why so many Negro applicants, rated favourably by the agency on first contact, dropped out after showing this initial interest in adoption. The greatest fall out came after the first interview, but some were put off by the unwelcoming voice of a clerk when they first rang to inquire about adoption. The researchers found these people were discouraged by any inhibition or lack of spontaneity in the person representing the agency. They came back only if rapport had been established in the very first contact with the agency. They were concerned about the possibility of prejudice, and were put off by such administrative requirements as completing forms and giving references on first contact, and on the need to establish their infertility with medical tests and reports. Fortunately, most agencies have got away from the establishment of infertility, as couples who can and often do have natural-born children are now coming to use adoption as a way of adding to their family. Yet some agencies continue to have administrative requirements such as completing an application form during the first interview, contacting referees or requiring applicants to have medical examinations before any real rapport has been established between the applicants and the agency. Such procedures are seen by many applicants as bureaucratic red tape and they are self defeating for the agency.

In a multi-racial society such as exists in Britain today, it is an adoption agency's job to find homes for all children who need them, regardless of racial or nationality background, and to give a professional service to all those concerned with the adoption. This is possible only if we understand the people we are trying to help. But this involves first understanding ourselves, the feelings and motivations that keep us from serving these people as well as we should do. Just rearranging our prejudices will not do. We must acknowledge them and then take a fresh look at these people we are trying to understand.

REFERENCES

(1) Rowe, Jane, *Parents, Children and Adoption*, Routledge & Kegan Paul, London, 1966, p. 181.
(2) Bernard, Viola, 'Application of Psychoanalytic Concepts to Adoption

F

Practice', *Psychoanalysis and Social Work*, 1953, International University Press.

(3) See Introduction for availability of the Adopters' Medical Form used by the British Adoption Project.

(4) Lusk, Janet, 'Co-operation between Doctors and Social Workers in Adoption', *Child Adoption*, No. 53, 1968, pp. 33–42 discusses this point fully.

(5) Stone, F. H., 'Adoption and Identity', *Child Adoption*, No. 58, 1968.

(6) Michaels, Ruth, 'Casework Considerations in Rejecting the Adoption Application', *Readings in Adoption*, I, by Evelyn Smith, Philosophical Library Inc. New York 1963, p. 305.

(7) Kirk, David H., *Shared Fate*, The Free Press, New York; and Collier-Macmillan Ltd, London, 1964.

(8) Menlove, Frances Lee, 'Aggressive Symptoms in Emotionally Disturbed Adopted Children', *Child Development*, Vol. 36, No. 2, June 1965.

(9) Block, Julia B., 'The White Worker and the Negro Client in Psychotherapy', *Social Work* (usa), Vol. 13, No. 2, April 1968.

(10) Kinnibrugh, A. D., *The Social Background of Immigrant Children from Asia and Cyprus*, Occasional Paper No. 1, Institute of Education, University of Leeds 1967 (limited circulation), pp. 39–46.

(11) Child Welfare League of America, *Standards for Adoption Service (Revised)*, C.W.L.A., New York, 1968.

(12) Lawder, Elizabeth, *et. al*, *A Followup Study of Adoptions*, Child Welfare League of America, New York, 1969.

(13) Fanshel, David, *A Study in Negro Adoption*, Child Welfare League of America, New York, 1957.

CHAPTER 5

THE PEOPLE WHO APPLIED TO ADOPT
A CHILD –
A STUDY OF THEIR CHARACTERISTICS

The Factual Study

The Project staff put a great deal of effort into an attempt to establish and measure some criteria for predicting which of the applicants could be expected to become 'successful' adoptive parents. Like numerous other people who have studied this problem, we finally had to admit that in the present state of our knowledge we were unable to point to any one factor as the most important in achieving a successful adoption. Nor did it prove possible to make a list of the necessary factors and weigh them in order of importance. To try to apply some criteria to interracial adoption was even more frustrating. Although we believed that a marginally satisfactory home would not be adequate to withstand the probable stress of bringing up an adopted child of different race, it was hard to say exactly what additional positive qualities these adopters would need to have. The staff and committee had ideas about this, of course, or they could not have gone ahead with the work, but it proved impossible to pinpoint and define the qualities clearly enough to measure them by research methods.

Finally, it was decided not to try to make any prediction in relation to specific criteria, but to do the best job we could in selecting adoptive parents, and then use the case files to learn what these people had in common and how they differed from those people who had applied but had not taken a child through the Project. This meant studying the characteristics of the consecutive series of 128 couples who (i) attended a pre-application group meeting, (ii) filled in and signed an application form, and (iii) got as far as having at least one interview with a social worker at the Project office. It was impossible to include the many others who inquired, since information about most of them was too limited. In fact, some comparisons had to be omitted because the amount of information about the people who applied and then withdrew, or were rejected, varied with the number of interviews before a decision was made. It was decided to keep to factual information of the kind that would not be subject to individual interpretation. This meant studying the circumstances of the applicants with a view to learning how much these entered into the adoption decision. We do not know whether the characteristics of our small group of adopters are representative of the people who adopt non-white children in Britain, as there is no other group of these adopters for comparison.

Adoption workers will not be surprised that in this factual study little difference was found in the circumstances of the successful and unsuccessful applicants, because adoption decisions (whether made by the applicants themselves or by the agency) are likely to depend on far more subtle factors than these. This finding led us to further study of the reasons for rejection or withdrawal, as well as to a quest for any positive qualities that had been found generally among the successful applicants but not to the same extent in the unsuccessful. These qualities were much more elusive than the facts and circumstances, and we were not able to measure them, but they are included here because the picture of the Project applicants would be completely inadequate without them. We are not making any predictions here about the outcome of the adoptions in relation to these qualities, but the very fact that children were placed with people who had these characteristics was, in effect, a prediction of their ability to integrate one of these children into their family.

First let us consider the factual study.

1. *background; family composition; source of referral*
The Project had applications from 105 white couples and twenty-three other couples. Eleven, or practically half of the non-white applicants became adoptive parents compared with two out of five of the white couples, so it can be said that the non-whites were somewhat more likely than the whites to complete their application successfully and go on to adopt. This is quite different from the high withdrawal rate found among Negro applicants by Fanshel in a study in Pittsburgh, Pennsylvania in 1957[1] and more recently by Bradley in another American city.[2]

TABLE 5.1

Race and Previous Parental Status of 51 Adoptive Couples

	White	Non-white	Mixed racial marriage	Total
Childless	8	5	4	17
Parents	32	0	2	34
Total:	40	5	6	51

TABLE 5.2

Race and Previous Parental Status of 77 Unsuccessful Applicants

	White	Non-white	Mixed racial marriage	Total
Childless	17	6	5	28
Parents	48	0	1	49
Total:	65	6	6	77

Among the Project applicants, childless couples and those with children were equally likely to be accepted. Nearly two out of every three applicants had children, though nearly all of these were white couples. All the couples where both husband and wife were of minority race were childless, but three of those with a mixed racial marriage had one child. Only a very small number of applicants had fostered or already adopted a child. None of the successful applicants had other adopted children, possibly because it is customary for adopters to return for the second child to the agency that placed the first child. Only one out of four in each group (successful or unsuccessful) had ever been considered for a child from another agency, thus refuting the commonly held idea that people seeking a coloured child are likely to be those who already have been refused a white child. However, half the accepted applicants had heard of the Project from some other social agency; many had written to International Social Service in connection with the Hong Kong Project, which by that time had all but ended; the others were referred to the British Adoption Project by local authorities or voluntary agencies that did not then place children for adoption, or at least not children of other races. Most of the other families read about the Project in the national daily newspapers, but as nearly all of these were white families this suggests that the reading habits of Britain's non-white population need to be explored, if agencies hope to use the press to interest them in adoption.

2. age and health of applicants

The age of Project applicants was very similar for those who went on to adopt and for those who did not. This was true for both husbands and wives, though the adoptive fathers did tend to be a little older than the unsuccessful male applicants, fewer of them being under thirty. Only one adoptive father and two other male applicants were over forty-five years old. There were no adoptive mothers and only three other wives over forty-five. The percentage of applicants between forty and forty-five years old was about 12 per cent of each group. It should be remembered that extremes of youth and age already had been eliminated through correspondence and group meetings. It is perhaps interesting to note that the wife was older than the husband in about one out of five applications, and that this was true for both groups of applicants, while the wife is older than the husband in only about one in eight marriages in England and Wales.[3] About one in five adopters had suffered some fairly serious illness but was now considered by the family doctor to have normal life expectancy. One in four of the unsuccessful applicants reported a past serious illness, although this was not always the reason the application was not accepted. We wonder if perhaps other medical problems might have been noted if every application had been continued to the point of having a medical examination.

3. religion; education; employment; socio-economic status

Three out of four applicants were at least nominally Christian, but we do not have information to go beyond that in describing the religious affiliation of those who did not adopt. Seventy individual adopters were Christian, many of them actively involved with their church. The Church of England, the Roman Catholic Church and various non-conformist faiths were represented. Five adopters were Muslim, one was Jewish and the remaining twenty-six individuals had no religious affiliation.

Both husbands and wives in the overall group of applicants were much better educated than the general population. Less than a third of the men in each of the groups we studied had left school at fifteen, which was in sharp contrast to the 80 per cent of the male population in England and Wales who left school at fourteen or fifteen. There was a somewhat higher percentage of successful than unsuccessful applicants who remained in school beyond the age of eighteen. The percentage of academic degrees was virtually the same for both groups of husbands, but there was a higher proportion of technical qualifications among the adoptive fathers. Just over half the adoptive fathers (including nearly half the non-European fathers) had a degree or its equivalent, but so did 43 per cent of the male applicants who did not go on to adoption. This is very different from the 3·7 per cent of men in England and Wales who continued full time education until the age of twenty or longer.[4]

In more than a third of the couples, both husband and wife had a qualification. Among the adoptive mothers just over half had a qualification, more of these being technical than academic. Just over a quarter of the wives in the unsuccessful group also had a qualification, but in their case the proportion of academic degrees was higher than the proportion with technical training.

Forty-one per cent of the adoptive mothers were employed at the time of applying to the Project, as against 26 per cent of the wives of the unsuccessful applicants, but except in one or two instances the income of the working wives was small, and it was the husband's income that was counted on to support the family. Income of husbands ranged from slightly less than £800 per annum to over £4,000, and the two applicants with the highest and lowest incomes were among those who became adoptive parents. The most usual income was £1,000 to £1,500, making up 43 per cent of the adopters and 35 per cent of the other applicants. This income seems low for a group well above average in education. Does it perhaps confirm our social workers' evaluation of the applicants as people who are more interested in doing work they enjoy than in competing for higher salaries? Or perhaps salary level is related to the fact that these men had spent many years qualifying and had not yet reached their maximum income. This is interesting inasmuch as our figures for the adopters (they are not available for the others) show them to be people who had been upwardly mobile, who were now in a higher occupational and social group than their father or their wife's father. Twenty-three of the men who adopted a child through the Project were in the Registrar General's Social Class I (professional and managerial), but the fathers of only two of these men were in that same grouping. Virtually half the families from which adopters and their wives had come were in

Social Class III, that is their fathers had been routine office or skilled manual workers. In over half the couples who adopted, both husband and wife had been upwardly mobile, and this may have contributed to their generally confident attitude to life. Almost half the adopters, and just over a quarter of the unsuccessful applicants, were in Social Class I in contrast to only one man in twenty in the population in London and the South-Eastern Region, where most of these families live.[5] It would be interesting to know if the dual nature of the Project – research and service – encouraged people in the professions or in management to apply, or whether the experience of other adoption agencies also shows a disproportionate number of people in Social Class I seeking to adopt non-white children. As people from many walks of life may make good adoptive parents, and children for adoption do not all fit well into one type of home, one hopes that people of various social and occupational groups will apply.

TABLE 5.3

Social Class of 51 Male Adopters Compared with Their Fathers

| | Adopters status category | | | | | | |
	Class I	Class II	Class III	Class IV	Class V	Total	%*
Higher than father	21	7	4	—	—	32	63
Lower than father	—	—	3	4	—	7	14
Same as father	2	5	4	1	—	12	23
Total:	23	12	11	5	—	51	100

* Percentages corrected to the nearest whole figure.

In the United States, Maas[6] found that children who were physically, ethnically or psychologically different tended to be adopted by people who were older, married longer and of lower educational and occupational status. However, most of the adoptions in the Maas study were not interracial, as the great majority of the children described as ethnically different were Negro children adopted by people of their own race. Fanshel's current study of ninety-seven American Indian children adopted by white American families found that over one-third of the adoptive fathers were in professional or managerial positions and another 16 per cent were secondary professionals.[7] A Project in the placement of Negro children in Toronto, Canada,[8] found that 42 per cent of its adopters (three-quarters of whom were white families) were in professional or managerial positions, and it was characteristic of them that they had confidence in themselves and in the future. In Montreal,[9] interracial adopters at the Children's Service Centre have been described as predominantly well-educated, intelligent and from professional groups who were active in church or community circles.

4. applicants' living accommodation and community

Three-quarters of the Project adopters were buying their home, as were well over half the unsuccessful applicants. The proportion of home-owners among the adopters was a good deal higher than for the general population in England and Wales among whom $46 \cdot 3$ per cent were reported as home-owners in the 1961 Census. Nearly half the adopters and at least as large a proportion of the other applicants lived in a semi-detached house. Only two adopters had a flat and one of these moved into a house as soon as a child was placed. All except one of the eleven non-white adopters were buying their own home, and that couple had a flat provided by the hospital which employed the adoptive father. Twice as many applicants lived in the outer London boroughs as in any one other local government unit within the Project's fifty-mile restriction. However, it was twice as usual for the adopters to live outside cities and within an urban or rural district council as for the unsuccessful applicants to do so.

Only one in five adopters lived in a neighbourhood that they described as not predominantly white. Unfortunately, the racial composition of the areas in which the unsuccessful applicants lived was not always known. Even among the non-European adopters, only one in three lived in a community that they considered less than predominantly white, and two families were the only non-whites in their neighbourhood. Some agencies have felt that a child should not be placed in an area where he is the only youngster or very nearly the only one who is racially different. However, the Toronto project mentioned above found the children had been better accepted in racially homogeneous areas than in mixed areas. Maas,[10] in his study of the successful adoptive parent applicant in nine different communities in the United States, also concluded that in the more homogeneous communities a child's ethnic difference seemed less threatening. We do not know how valid these conclusions would be in Britain, but recent studies by the Institute of Race Relations, London, found less prejudice among people who lived in the same area with people of other races.[11]

In any case, it is very doubtful whether the type of community should be a deciding factor in placing a baby or young child for adoption, as the geographical mobility of the population and the changes occurring in many communities are likely to upset any such planning. As evidence of this, in 1969 eighteen of the Project's fifty-one adoptive parents were no longer living at the address from which they originally applied to the Project. Two of the families were living abroad and two others had moved to the north of England. None had moved because the neighbourhood was uncongenial; they had moved because they wanted a larger house or better school and play facilities.

5. *marriage; size of family; age of children*

The length of time adopters have been married is one of those factors in an application that often gives rise to a rule based only on the personal experience of social workers, committee members, judges or guardians *ad litem*. The Project tried to be flexible about this point, but the figures show that three out of four who were accepted had been married three to ten years. Few couples who had been married less than three years went on to become adoptive parents. This was a second marriage for one in ten of those who adopted, as well as for those who did not, so the number of marriages was not a determinant of a successful outcome to the application. This was a first marriage for all the non-European applicants.

TABLE 5.4

Length of Marriage of Successful and Unsuccessful Applicants

	Adopters	(%)*	Unsuccessful applicants	(%)*
Under 3 years	3	(6)	11	(14)
3 to 6 years	18	(35)	21	(27)
6 to 10 years	21	(41)	20	(26)
10 years plus	9	(18)	25	(33)
Total:	51	100	77	100

* Percentages corrected to the nearest whole figure.

There was no significant difference in the size of the families in the two groups being studied. Only one successful applicant and a very few of the unsuccessful had children by a former marriage, but two out of three applicants in both groups had children of their present marriage. Most of these had only one or two children, but there were seven couples who had four children, and one with five children, and three of the couples who already had four children became parents to an adopted child as well. One in five applicants in each group had suffered a miscarriage, stillbirth or neo-natal death, and a few families had experienced this more than once.

TABLE 5.5

Number of Children of Present Marriage

Number of children	Adopters	(%)*	Unsuccessful applicants	(%)*
None	17	(33)	28	(36)
One	14	(27)	22	(29)
Two	12	(24)	12	(16)
Three	5	(10)	10	(13)
Four	3	(6)	4	(5)
Five	0	—	1	(1)
Total:	51	100	77	100

* Percentages corrected to nearest whole figure.

Many applicants wished to keep to a minimum the difference in age between their youngest biological child and the adopted baby. Sometimes they felt they were letting the older child down if he passed eighteen months of age without a new brother or sister. This had to be balanced against the parents' ability to satisfy the rather special needs of an adopted baby without the other youngster, who also was essentially a baby, feeling his special place in the family had been usurped by a newcomer. This was made more complicated by the fact that the adopted baby was not a newborn, but a developing personality that the older child must relate to. In one or two instances the Project placed a child closer in age than seemed desirable. This was due to a baby's urgent need for a family, which made us hope the adopters would be able to stretch their capacities to meet the need of both children for a great deal of attention. Our records show that the youngest child already in a family, when an adopted child was placed, was fifteen months old and the newcomer was three months. There were eight families in which the youngest child was twenty months to two years old when the adopted baby was placed, and ten families in which the youngest child was two years to two years and eight months.

However, the age of the adopted children at placement varied, with the result that the shortest age gap was only eight months and the next shortest was nine months. We found that an age difference of less than a year made the adjustment much more difficult for all concerned and we cannot recommend it.

6. *age, sex and race of child requested*
No difference between the two groups of applicants emerges from a comparison of the sort of child requested. Age, sex and race of the child the applicants wanted apparently had little to do with whether an application was accepted and a child was placed. Three out of five applicants in each group asked for an Asian or Anglo-Asian child, while one in five requested a Negro or part-Negro child of African or West Indian background, and another one in five said they had no preference. Unfortunately, the way the question was worded on the application form made it seem that a preference was expected, which almost certainly influenced the requests to some extent.

Half of each group of applicants wanted a child under six months of age, most of them specifying 'as young as possible'. Nearly a fifth of each group asked for a child of 'any age'. A somewhat larger percentage of the adopters than of the other group wanted a child *over* a certain specified age, e.g. over six months or over nine months. Just over half the adopters and somewhat less than half of the unsuccessful applicants wanted a girl. Just under one-third in each group asked for a boy. The remainder merely sought to adopt a child and had no preference as to sex.

7. *summary of findings*
The overall group of applicants showed certain characteristics which can be summarized as follows, but little difference was found in the situations of those who adopted and those who did not.

The applicants had not gone the rounds of the agencies seeking a white child. They were specifically interested in taking a non-European child.

These were not people who had already adopted or fostered a child.

One in five of the wives was older than her husband.

Three out of four individual applicants, both successful and otherwise, were Christians. The Project also accepted as adopters a fairly large number of applicants who had well defined ethical and moral values but no religious affiliation.

The percentage of applicants with a degree or an equivalent qualification was far higher than in the general population.

Families with incomes ranging from under £800 to over £4,000 a year applied to adopt a child, but well over a third earned between £1,000 and £1,500 per annum.

More than a third of all applicants, and nearly half of those who became adoptive parents, were in the Registrar General's Social Class I (professional and managerial).

Two-thirds of the adopters were in a higher social and occupational group than their parents, virtually half of whom were in Social Class III (skilled manual occupations and routine office work).

The applicants were much more likely than the man in the street to be buying a home, usually a three-bedroom, semi-detached house in an outer London borough. Proportionately, still larger numbers of non-white applicants were buying their own home, most of them a terraced house in one of the inner London boroughs.

Both white and non-white adopters tended to live in a predominantly white neighbourhood. This information was not known for the unsuccessful applicants.

By the end of the four-year Project, one in three of the adopters had moved house, leading us to believe that with so much mobility the ethnic composition of the community into which a non-white baby is placed may not be of much importance.

Four out of five applicants had a preference as to the race of the child they wanted to adopt. Most often they wanted a child of Asian or Anglo-Asian parentage.

Non-European applicants were childless, as were also most of the racially-mixed applicants.

White applicants most often had one or more natural-born children, the youngest under five years old.

Applicants who had been married less than three years or more than ten years, or where the husband was under thirty, were less likely to become adoptive parents.

Principal Reasons for Rejection or Withdrawal
As the above study failed to show enough difference to explain why some applicants went on to adopt and others did not, we explored the reasons why the seventy-seven unsuccessful applicants withdrew or were rejected, as recorded at the time the action was taken. The *principal* reasons for withdrawal or rejection were categorized as shown in Table 5.6, but in some cases several reasons contributed to the decision. No attempt has been made to separate the rejected from the withdrawn applications, as often there were elements of both in a decision. Some applicants were helped to withdraw; others did so without encouragement. Some were rejected who might have been expected to withdraw, but did not do so, perhaps preferring to place the responsibility on the Project team for their failure to get a child.

TABLE 5.6

Principal Reasons for Withdrawal and Rejection of Applications

Problems of personality and mental health	26
Pregnancy	14
Conflict of interests and/or poor timing	6
Offered child by another agency	5
Decided to have biological child	5
Relatives seriously anti-adoption or anti-colour	5
Moved out of area	3
Serious problems of physical health	3
Not united in wish to adopt	3
Transferred their application to another agency	2
Lapsed (reason unknown)	2
Unresolved religious conflict	1
Financial reverse	1
Preferred third party adoption	1
Total:	77

In Table 5.6, the category 'Problems of personality and mental health' includes several applicants with a history of mental or emotional illness, and two whose personality problems had brought them into serious conflict with the law. Some of the other personality and mental health problems were: a depressive outlook on life; inability to withstand stress; unresolved feelings about early deprivation; considerable anxiety; impotence; tenseness; perfectionism; lack of warmth; inability to express or communicate feelings; an intellectual or superficial approach; marital disharmony; a limited awareness of the needs of adopted children and particularly non-white adopted children.

The category 'Conflict of interests and/or poor timing' includes families that the Project felt were already fully stretched with the responsibilities they were carrying. They had a career or hobby, or some responsibility (e.g. fostering several children or one child with serious problems) that would conflict with the care of an adopted child, who could only be sandwiched in between these other interests. It also includes some very young families who had not yet finished their career training, or who already had a young baby, and some other families whose lives seemed completely full without another child, or where this did not seem a good time to add an adopted baby to the family. Some of these applicants probably could have been classified as personality problems because of their impulsiveness, or a tendency to be unrealistic, or to move rapidly from one new interest to another. Adoption is such a long-term undertaking that we felt some of these people were insufficiently motivated to carry their interest in the adopted child for the necessary number of years. In other cases it seemed likely that an adopted child would ultimately prove too great a burden. Some of the applicants, after thoroughly considering adoption, decided to have a baby of their own. Others who became pregnant while their application was being considered expressed disappointment not to be able to adopt at this time.

We shall never know whether these applicants had more potential than we thought for being adoptive parents to a non-European child, but decisions had to be made, as they always do, by using one's best judgement in the light of the knowledge available at the time. Our aim was that recommended by the Hurst Committee, namely to provide protection for children from being adopted by 'people unsuited to the responsibility, and for adopters from undertaking responsibilities for which they were not fitted, or which they had not appreciated'.[12]

Positive Qualities in Accepted Applicants

After reviewing the reasons why applications had been rejected or withdrawn from the Project, the staff decided to see whether there were any qualities common to all or many of the adopters, and whether these qualities were found among the other applicants as well or were unique to the successful applicants. According to the case files the following qualities were found to be descriptive of the adopters, though of course not equally in every case. Some of the other applicants also had been described as having a number of these qualities, but it had been necessary to reject the application for some other reason, as already shown in Table 6. No attempt was made to assign weight to these positive qualities, or to list them in order of their importance.

Qualities Found in Accepted Applicants

Positive attitudes towards people and acceptance of their differences.

Loving and supportive relationships within the marriage and family.

Open personality that can communicate feelings easily.

Enjoyment of life.[13]

Ability to benefit from experience.

Enjoyment of children as individuals.

Faith in themselves and in the future (this could also be stated as enough emotional security to take some risks in life).

Ability to enlist the support of close relatives or friends.

These qualities were found as generously among the Project's non-European adopters, who took a child of their own racial background, as they were among the couples who adopted across racial lines. Whether these characteristics are found quite generally among adopters, or even among interracial adopters, we do not know. We can only say they were conspicuous among the Project's adoptive parents. We hope they may be factors that will be correlated with success in integrating the adopted child into their family in a way that will be satisfying to them and to the child, but only research with these families in the years ahead can determine this.

Dr Judd Marmor,[14] speaking to the National Conference on Social Welfare (USA) in 1964, said experience in Canada and the United States showed that families adopting 'trans-racially' shared certain common characteristics of self-confidence, self-awareness and a light touch and that they fall into a group of the population who are unusually free from tendencies towards ethnocentrism, i.e. they do not think in terms of in-group or out-group hierarchies, but tend to evaluate people on their objective merits as human beings regardless of race, religion or other group identifications. Although we have described them in somewhat different terms, the positive qualities of the Project adopters include the characteristics Dr Marmor found.

From time to time we have heard the suggestion that anyone 'virtuous' enough to want to take a non-white child should be given one. Some have said the 'marginal' applicant, who might not be appropriate for a normal, healthy young English baby, might still be offered a child of different race, or perhaps an older or handicapped white child. The rationalization for this view is that such children are likely to live out their childhood in a Children's Home, or in one or more foster homes, and that the marginal adoptive home may be better than growing up with no family ties at all. In fact, it appears that the child who is different, and therefore harder to place, often does get the marginal home if he gets a home at all. Trudy Bradley's[15] recent detailed research, into how caseworkers in one large American city perceived their adoptive applicants, found that they were unlikely to place the 'burden' of a child who was different on the couples they regarded most positively. Dr Bradley thinks there probably were psychological reasons why caseworkers did this but it might also mean that workers were incorporating some aspects of the value system of the community, values that are not likely to be wholly accepting of the child who is different. Dr Kellmer Pringle reports that Shapiro in 1957 and Kadushin in 1962, in American studies, found that so-called hard-to-place children are more often given to applicants who are only marginally eligible as adoptive parents.[16] In Britain social workers have told us that families not thought entirely suitable as adoptive applicants sometimes are used as foster parents for children placed 'with a view to adoption', and such children are often those with a placement problem of race, age or health. Our national survey reported in Chapter 10 found that people adopting a non-white child in Britain

G

were more than three times as likely as other adopters to have first fostered the child.

The Project staff and committee felt that bringing up a non-white adopted child in Britain today would call for the very best adoptive parents, since these children are likely to have even more need than other adopted children for acceptance and security. Also, we were conscious that interracial adoption in Britain was to some extent on trial, and the demonstration would not be a fair one unless the adopters were considered to be thoroughly competent for the task.

Our study of the applicants has shown that the differences between the circumstances of the adopters and of the unsuccessful applicants were too few in number and in degree to explain why some went on to adopt a child through the Project and others did not. Reviewing earlier follow up research projects in Britain and North America, Dinnage says, 'It does not seem that the adopters' age, income or religion or the presence of other children in the home, makes a decisive difference to the outcome of the adoption except in the context of many other factors'.[17] Her report goes on to say that 'no other circumstances of adoption (except possibly the child's pre-placement experience) is so important as the kind of people the adopters are, and the kind of family life they are able to create'. We feel sure this is true – perhaps even more so – when the child and the adopters are of different race.

REFERENCES

(1) Fanshel, David, *A Study in Negro Adoption*, Child Welfare League of America, New York, 1957, pp. 61–9.
(2) Bradley, Trudy, *An Exploration of Caseworkers' Perception of Adoptive Applicants*, Child Welfare League of America, New York, 1967, pp. 61, 173 and 174.
(3) *Registrar General's Statistical Review of England and Wales for the Year 1967*, Part II, p. 57.
(4) *Census 1961: England and Wales*, 'Education Tables', HMSO, 1966, p. 87.
(5) *Census 1961: England and Wales*, 'Occupational Tables', p. 193.
(6) Maas, Henry S., 'The Successful Adoptive Parent Applicant', *Social Work* (USA), Vol. 5, No. 1, January 1960, p. 20.
(7) Fanshel, David, privileged communication.
(8) Social Planning Council of Metropolitan Toronto, *The Adoption of Negro Children: a Community-wide Approach*, Toronto, 1966, pp. 44, 49.

(9) Marmor, Judd, 'Psychodynamic Aspects of Trans-Racial Adoptions', *Social Work Practice*, National Conference on Social Welfare (USA), 1964, p. 6.

(10) ibid, p. 20.

(11) Rose, E. J. B., *et al.*, *Colour and Citizenship*, Institute of Race Relations, London, 1969.

(12) *Report of the Departmental Committee on the Adoption of Children*, HMSO, 1954, p. 4.

(13) Lawder, Elizabeth, *et al.*, *Follow up Study of Adoptions*, Child Welfare League of America, New York, 1969, stresses the importance of this quality, which she calls 'joie de vivre'.

(14) Marmor, *op. cit.*, p. 6.

(15) Bradley, *op. cit.*, p. 189.

(16) Kellmer Pringle, M. L., *Adoption: Facts and Fallacies*, Longmans, London, 1966, p. 28.

(17) Dinnage, Rosemary, 'Research on Adoption', *Case Conference*, Vol. 13, No. 10, February 1967, pp. 357-60.

CHAPTER 6

PLACEMENT OF A CHILD

Choosing a Family for a Child
The day the adoptive parents take the baby home and he begins a new life with them is the high point in the adoption process; after this even the court hearing comes as something of an anticlimax. One after another of the adopters told us this in the post adoption interviews and discussion groups.

Who decided to offer this child to this particular family, and what entered into this far reaching decision? In the Project, as in most agencies, placement was a shared responsibility, and because of the size of the Project this involved the whole staff. The suggestion for a combination of child and family could come from the director or one of the workers, but the decision to recommend the placement to the case committee was made only after the staff had met and agreed to this move. The Adoption Act 1958 requires the agency's case committee to approve each placement, but surely it is the duty of the professional staff to make a strong recommendation and to support it with enough relevant information to enable the committee to make a wise decision.

The whole matter of so-called 'matching' of child and family arises at this point. What is meant by matching and how is it done? Do we really mean matching or is this a misleading word for describing what adoption workers try to do? The word always recalls to the author's mind an interviewer several years ago, who told her applicants all about her agency's efforts to match children and adopters, then followed this up by asking if they would be willing to take a very dull child! What are we trying to match? To be more specific, let us consider this process in the work of the Project. At no time was a home used for a child because the adopters' name had come to the top of a waiting list, but only when the home seemed able to meet the needs of a particular child. Sometimes the choice had to be made from a very small number of approved homes because of the small size of the programme. The basis for selecting a home for a child was an appraisal of their suitability for each other, and most unfortunately, when no reasonably suitable combination was available, the baby had to wait.

Age, sex and religion usually were the first factors considered, though religion was included only if the natural mother had exercised her right to specify a particular religion. It was felt the child needed a home where he would be welcomed as he was, where no one would need to pretend or treat him like a tiny and completely dependent baby, if in reality he was a crawler or a toddler already investigating everything in the house. He required a home, too, where he would find it good to be a boy or a girl as the case might be, and where as he grew older he could develop his sexual identity with pride; he needed a family where his developing masculinity or femininity would not become a threat to one of his parents, and they would not have to act out through him their own struggle with parental authority. The Project wanted to know which adopters could happily accept and meet the needs of an older infant and which could only feel truly parental towards a child they had cared for as a tiny baby. The real wishes of the family about the sex of the child, and the underlying reasons for any strong preference, had been explored during the family study, and they were taken into consideration in deciding on the home for a particular child. The location of the adoptive home, in relation to where the natural parents and foster parents were living, and the area from which the child had originated were considered, so that the child would not be placed in his home area, where the adopters might accidentally meet former parents or foster parents.

Whatever other factors may enter into suitability when agencies are choosing a specific home for a child, in the Project there was always the added factor of race. Most families were not equally ready or able to accept into their family (especially into the extended family) a child of *any* race or combination of races. Most favoured some racial characteristics over others, this being even more true of the non-European and racially-mixed adopters, most of whom sought a child like themselves while some wanted a lighter child. The families often could accept one kind of difference but not another and, since their genuine acceptance of the adopted child was so important, this factor had to be considered in selecting adopters for each child. This was not matching in the sense of parents and children being similar, but it was taking into consideration the child's need to be accepted as he was, and the adopters' ability to accept specific differences in appearance due to racial background. The needs of a child who happened to be light in colour occasionally resulted in a family taking a lighter child than they had envisaged, with other children in the family expressing some disappointment after they had been prepared for a 'brown' sister or brother.

The first meeting with the baby is the time when he becomes real for prospective adopters. Until then they have had only a mental image of him. This meeting might be expected to be even more of a moment of truth when the adopters and child are of different races, yet our experience has not shown any hesitation by these adopters in expressing their delight with the baby and their feeling that he was right for their family. It not only seemed that way at the meeting, but also upon serious reflection some months or a year or two later. The only adopters, who decided not to take the first child they met, were a couple from the Caribbean to whom we offered a baby older than they sought and towards whom they did not feel drawn. A little later they took a child that was younger and more like them, and they immediately felt he was right for them. Adoption workers in Britain still have much to learn about the meaning that various degrees of colour, certain facial features, hair, and the ethnic background of a child may have for non-European adopters as individuals and as members of their racial group.

The expectations of the adopters were considered in other areas as well as age, sex and race, since it seems that adopted children even more than biological children do not want to fail their parents. Thirty per cent of the adoptive parents in a recent study[1] seemed to be either over-ambitious, exerting undue pressure on their child to do well at school, or were disappointed at his lack of achievement. One hopes adoptive parents will not need to use their child's achievement to convince themselves or others that adoption is a good way of having a family. Yet even in natural families much is expected of the eldest child, while dependence and under achievement may be well accepted or even encouraged in the youngest child. This caused us to consider the adopted child's place in the family and what would be expected of him in that role.

In placing very young babies it is difficult if not impossible to predict the temperament and personality of the child in later years. Whether temperament is an inborn characteristic or entirely acquired has been the subject of much conjecture, but the question is still unanswered. Very young babies may be generally placid, fretful, sensitive or very active, but whether these qualities are congenital or are the baby's response to the first mothering experience is not known. The Project felt these characteristics should be taken into consideration, when choosing a family for a child, to the extent that the adopters should be able to understand and cope with a youngster of that particular temperament, instead of depending upon his changing later in response to their care. In those of the children who were somewhat older, the temperament and personality of the child and the adopters were considered of great importance to the outcome of the placement and were carefully evaluated. This is not to say they necessarily were alike and 'matched', but rather there was reason to think they would be able to understand and accept each other. Even an older child might change a good deal in due course, but it seemed unwise to count on this.

Today there is much less emphasis on matching in adoption than there was some years ago when agencies felt more confidence in being able to predict a baby's future intelligence and personality. The findings of Brenner's follow up study of five-year-olds in 1948 discouraged the use of infant testing as a means of predicting later intelligence.[2] This added to the impetus already given to early placement in the work of Bowlby, Spitz and others, since one of the principal reasons for delaying placement had been to predict later intellectual ability. With the advent of adoption placement directly from the hospital or in the first few weeks of life, placements had to be made with very little, if anything, known about the baby himself except pre-natal, birth and neo-natal history. This called for adopters who were willing to take greater risks. Actually adopters had been asking to accept these risks for some time, and many had bypassed the agencies by taking a child through a third party in order to have a very young baby. So in some agencies there has been a movement away from matching and toward placing young babies with adopters who are willing to take this kind of risk. This change has become much more general practice in North America, and the 1968 revision of the *Child Welfare League of America: Standards for Adoption Service*[3] states:

'The ability of adoptive parents to accept the child as he is or as he may later develop, regardless of how he may differ from them, is of greater importance than similarity of characteristics.'

It goes on to say, however, that people vary in their capacity to accept differences, and when it is important for adoptive parents to have a child they feel is like them, they should have a right both to express their wishes and have these taken into consideration.

Although placement is almost more an art than a science, adoption workers are forever being expected to foresee the future, to predict how people will behave in an untried situation, and the influences they will have upon one another in a new relationship. In the present state of our knowledge this cannot be an exact science. When a new person enters a family, all the old members must make some adjustment in their relationships to one another in order to include the new person, with the result that the whole configuration changes and will never be quite the same again. If the balance in relationships is too delicate, the coming of a new person into the nuclear family may be very upsetting indeed. As we have seen in Chapter 4, one of the aims of the family study is to evaluate the strength of these relationships and the likelihood of their being able to stand the strain of the addition of an unrelated child. The individual child's response to various members of his new family and their individual responses to him in living together as a family can only be conjectured.

Parental Consent and Committee Approval
As soon as the staff had decided they would like to offer a particular child to a family, whose application they had approved, a summary of the file on both child and family, along with a statement of the reasons for selecting this home for this child, was submitted to the case committee for approval. Early in the Project, combinations were not presented to the committee until the family had seen the child and decided they wanted him and the mother had signed her consent, but delays in getting the case committee together and in taking the mother's consent often meant considerable delay between the time a family saw a baby and the day they could take him home. To overcome this the committee agreed to approve the placements before the proposed adopters had met the child, and conditional only upon the mother's consent. Of course, a mother had already signed that she had read the legally required Memorandum, which explained her rights in relation to consent. Having the committee's approval of the placement made it possible to be more sensitive in the timing of consent and placement, which seemed to be in the best interest of all the parties involved.

When the mother was a married woman, her husband's consent to the adoption was secured, as required by most courts, even when he was not the father of this child. When the putative father was interested and available, he signed his consent as evidence of his agreement with the plan. Though the law does not require his consent to adoption, the court must consider a putative father's views when he is a respondent in the case. A putative father also has the right to apply for custody of the child under the Guardianship of Infants Act. We felt his signature to an adoption consent indicated the father's participation in and agreement with the planned adoption.

The next step was to secure a serial number by telephone from one of the courts in the area where the proposed adopters lived, most often the court used by the children's department. The adopters would be known by this serial number instead of by name on the consent form. The mother was told that adopters had now been found for the baby, so her plans for the child could go forward if she felt ready to sign her consent. Each mother already knew that our procedure was different from most agencies in this country in as much as we would require her consent before placing the baby in the adoption home, using her action in signing the consent form as a measure of the firmness of her decision. In an interview with her Project worker she was given some information about the proposed family without identifying them or the area in which they lived. Some mothers wished to know quite a bit about the adopters, others did not. Many expressed confidence that a suitable home had been selected and they wished to know only two or three things about the family, things that had especial meaning for the individual mother such as whether there were children in the family, if there was a dog or other pets, whether the family lived in the city or country. We left this to the mother, not pressing on her information she did not particularly want, but giving it more freely to those who wanted to be able to imagine their child in a specific environment.

Most of the Project mothers wanted their child to get settled in a permanent family as soon as possible and had been waiting for a home to be found, so they were quite ready to proceed with signing the consent. The adoption worker always went through the form very carefully with the mother to make sure she understood its full meaning. She explained the mother's legal position, reminding her that the law would allow her to change her mind until the legal adoption, but saying that the Project would regard her signature as proof of her considered and final decision, so she should sign only if completely ready to do so. To some mothers, at least, it seemed a relief to know her signature on the consent form was morally binding even if not legally so.

As mentioned in Chapter 3, a very large percentage of the Project mothers had made a final decision for adoption before the child was born and nearly nine out of ten had made it before the baby was six weeks old, so it was not strange that they were ready to give their final consent. This raises again the question of how long a mother requires to make a final decision about relinquishing all her parental rights and responsibilities towards her child, and whether she has not the right as well as the painful obligation to set her signature to a decision and call it final, without being harassed afterwards by repeated queries as to whether she is sure. No one would want a mother who is *not* sure to sign such a consent, but when her decision has been made and she is ready, she should know that the document is binding. If there is any question about a foreign mother's understanding of English, an interpreter should make the explanations. It was the opinion of the Project's legal adviser that when a mother does not read English she should sign a translation of the consent form in her own language, with the translation attested to by an Embassy or High Commission Official. This was done for one of the Project mothers.

The adoption worker usually accompanied the mother to the office of a county court when she went there to sign her consent, witnessed by an official of the court. Most mothers were glad to have the worker's support at this time. Unfortunately, the signing was often an undignified and casual procedure. Usually there was no private room, or when there was, it was made available only after the worker had requested it. Otherwise the mother had to stand at a public counter to sign the paper to relinquish her baby. Some clerks were offhand and unconcerned; to them it was a routine job of witnessing a signature. Sometimes they said nothing beyond, 'Sign here'; occasionally – not always by any means – they asked if the mother had read the form. With the foreign girls, especially, one might have expected them to want to be sure the mothers knew what they were signing. One or two joked about the difficulty of pronouncing or spelling Asian names, and another prattled on about the mistakes he had known colleagues to make when witnessing signatures. JPs, and some clerks, were more understanding and kindly; they made sure the mother knew she would have no further right to see the child after legal adoption, and reminded her that she could change her mind until an Adoption Order was made by the court. None mentioned the importance of the consent she was giving or what a late change of decision would mean to the child or the adopters.

In some cases the Project staff felt it was unfortunate that the mother could not give her final and legal consent to adoption when she was ready to do so, even though a family had not yet been found for the baby. This would involve signing a non-specific consent rather than a consent to adoption by a particular family. In many parts of Canada and the United States this is possible. There, the mother relinquishes her child to the adoption agency either directly or at a court hearing. If her petition is granted, the agency is given custody of the child with a right to consent to adoption without further notification to or involvement of the mother in the proceedings. If the child is found to be unadoptable, the placement agency is expected to take responsibility for more appropriate planning for the child, but in the case of small voluntary agencies the local authority often helps in this. Actually the British Adoption Act, 1958 (Section 35), designates the placement agency as the responsible body by placing an obligation on an agency to receive the child back, if he has to be withdrawn from adopters or if an Adoption Order is not made. If the agency can be held responsible for the child and his future at that stage, why not in the first instance when the mother first relinquishes her rights and responsibilities to her child?

Methods in Placement

The Project came to feel strongly that no specific child should be mentioned to possible adopters until: (i) the adopters' application had been approved; (ii) the adoption agency worker knew the child and he had been medically examined for adoption placement; (iii) parental consent had been signed or there was at least every reason to believe a firm and final decision had been made; (iv) all the appropriate staff members had been involved in the decision to offer this child to this family; (v) the case committee had approved the placement or there was at least every reason to expect the committee to do so. The Project took this stand after being less definite about the procedure in the first placements, which had included one verbal offer of three babies, causing the adopters unnecessary anxiety and concern about the two they could not take. Adopters are so vulnerable at this point, and so are babies and foster parents, that we cannot afford to 'leak' a possible placement until we are entirely sure we can go ahead with it if the prospective adopters want the child. In the case of older children any talk of possible adoption that then comes to nothing can be almost disastrous for the child. But premature confiding in adopters can be traumatic for them too. We talked with a couple who said an agency had suggested they would get one of three babies to be born in May, but May and June passed uneventfully and in July they were advised by letter that their application had not been accepted by the case committee. Another couple said an adoption agency had told them about a particular child before their application had been studied, then twice during the study the worker confided that the mother was very undecided and might keep the baby. When she did decide to relinquish the child, examination disclosed a rather serious medical condition. Clearly this was the wrong order of things. The agency was nowhere nearly ready to place this baby; the home was not ready either as the application had not yet been accepted. The result was that the prospective adopters were put through an unproductive emotional ordeal not unlike the experience of a pregnancy that ends in miscarriage or stillbirth.

When an application was accepted by the Project, a letter went out to the adopters to tell them this, and saying we would let them know as soon as there was a child we thought they would want to consider. If more than a few weeks elapsed between acceptance and offering the child, the worker tried to use this time to help the applicants develop their potentialities as adoptive parents, with the result that in most instances there was no long period of time without constructive contact between the family and the Project. Even so, one family became discouraged when a child was not offered and withdrew to apply elsewhere, but later withdrew from that agency because of its rigid requirements.

When a baby was ready for placement, it became the usual procedure to send prospective adopters some information about the baby and his background, which they could consider together before discussing it with their worker and before seeing the baby. In a few instances the worker decided to present the material orally for discussion, giving the adopters the information in writing to take home with them. If anything was worrying to them this was the best time to come to grips with it, before meeting an appealing baby. There is much difference of opinion among agencies about the kinds of information that should be given to adoptive parents and when it should be given. Some people feel 'everything' should be told; others believe only pertinent information that the adopters can use constructively should be given. It is easier to know what to give if we consider the reasons for giving any information at all. The Child Welfare League of America[4] suggests adoptive parents should be given information that would help them to:

(1) understand the child and his special needs and problems;
(2) decide whether they can accept him;
(3) understand and feel comfortable about the natural parents and the reasons they gave up the child for adoption;
(4) help the child understand about adoption.

The Project staff felt they had a professional responsibility to select the facts adopters would need for use in these four ways. We agreed, too, with Jane Rowe who suggests telling everything that will be helpful to the adopters, but not using the acceptance of sordid details as a sort of fitness test for adoptive parenthood.[5] She reminds us that adopters do not necessarily share social workers' attitudes to social problems and it is the workers' job to minimize, not increase, adopters' anxiety. David Kirk[6] writes of the importance of adopters accepting the child's background as not alien to their own values, so they can identify with the natural parents. He says that, if the child senses a distance between his adopters and his natural forebears, it makes it impossible to fuse the image of his natural and adoptive parents into a single configuration that is acceptable and satisfying to him. The social background of some children who can benefit from adoption is such that, if adopters were burdened with all the 'sins of the fore-fathers', it would be impossible for most adopters to see them as anything *but* alien to their own values. Actually, the Project was rarely asked to place a child with a very bad background, but we could not in any case have placed a child whose background was so questionable as to constitute a serious variable in the research, any more than we could place a child with a serious medical problem. If a child had a very serious problem in his background it would be hard to tell in the follow up studies whether adoptive parents were reacting to this or to the child's colour. This is not to deny the need of such children for a good home by adoption or the existence of people willing to adopt them.

We got as much pertinent background information as possible, but this was limited by the fact that the extended family or one of the child's parents usually was overseas and living in circumstances difficult to evaluate at a distance and from the viewpoint of a different culture. But even in local situations, social agencies by their very nature almost always know more about the problems and weaknesses than about the strengths of families. The 'everything' an agency knows is not likely to be a total picture of a child's background even in terms of social history, much less in terms of inherited character-istics, and the agency's particular focus may give a very distorted picture. One is likely to know only the present generation, or at most one more, but a child inherits from many ancestors.

As mentioned earlier, the Project made every effort to secure accurate and complete information about the child himself: his development, history, medical data, likes and dislikes, and his ways of responding to people. These facts were passed on to adopters. So was a general idea of the natural parents' appearance including their depth of colour, as we thought these children might be particularly interested in that in later years. The natural parents' education, health, general occupational grouping, major interests and specific abilities, as well as a general statement about why they gave up the baby for adoption, were all included in the carefully written material given to adopters. Workers tried to keep to facts and allow the adopters to make their own interpretations, so they avoided the use of such value words as beautiful, plain or abandoned in describing a child, or words like handsome, unreliable, uneducated, in relation to natural parents.

When a couple felt positively about the description of the child and his background, plans were made for them to see him and get to know him. We tried showing the child in his foster home, in his residential nursery, in the mother-and-baby home and at the Project office, and in most cases we found the office the most satisfactory. This was not because an office is well set up for babies, but because the agency had better control over the meeting and could adapt the procedure in individual situations. The people involved usually were limited to the baby, the adopters and the appropriate Project workers. We felt the adopters should not be confused by seeing younger, more appealing or apparently more needy children than the one being offered, and that they should be able to react freely to the child offered without the restraint occasioned by the consideration due to a foster mother or nursery matron who had had the care of the baby.

It also seemed better if the foster mother or matron did not add her interpretation of the natural mother to the one already given by the worker. For example, a foster mother or matron may interpret the mother's failure to visit the child as a sign of neglect or lack of interest, whereas the worker knows the mother has been preparing herself for the permanent separation from her child that adoption will mean for her. One foster mother had a very poor opinion of a young foreign-speaking mother, who always visited the baby accompanied by one of three different young men, all of whom actually were her brothers trying to show family solidarity and give moral support to their sister. Another difficulty in sending adopters alone to a nursery or foster home is that nursery staff and foster parents sometimes become so fond of their small charges that they become possessive towards them, and quite unconsciously they make the adopters feel incompetent and undeserving of the child. We do not wish to imply any criticism of the indispensable part these people play in child care, but they have their feelings, too, and are bound to react one way or another to the new parents, thus adding additional strong feelings to an already emotionally charged situation. Where an agency has its own foster homes or residential nurseries with people specializing in caring for pre-adoption babies, these caretakers may become part of the agency team and have a well-defined role to play in the placement process. The babies placed by the Project were in foster homes or nurseries of almost as many agencies as there were babies. They were not employed by us and often had experienced quite different methods of placement, so it was expecting a good deal of them to accept the Project's ways, but most of them tried very hard to work co-operatively with the staff in spite of this.

Even with quite young babies, we insisted on the adopters taking time – at least over night after meeting the baby – to be sure they felt this was a baby they could love and accept as a part of their family. When a baby was several months old at placement, it was accepted that more time would be needed for him to feel comfortable with his new parents and discover they knew how to care for him. This meant at least a second visit to the baby before the adopters took him home. We worked on the assumption that even young babies are sensitive to changes in the way they are handled, and that the older baby can be expected to grieve for his lost foster mother, yet in time will respond to comforting and the warmth of the new parents' affection. Meanwhile, a familiar routine and methods of care will help him to settle. The work of an American researcher (Schaffer) suggests that the lack of strong overt protest in a young baby cannot be taken as evidence that the baby is unaffected by the experience of separation and change.[7] Jean Charnley, in her book *The Art of Child Placement*, says babies are the most delicate and sensitive of humans, and the greatest mistake in social work is in crediting them with too little feeling. She goes on to say that in any separation there is a wound, but it can be treated in such a way that it will leave only a little scar, and that babies have within them, as all people do in varying degrees, an ability to take pain and find a way of living with it.[8]

The older a child, the more preparation we felt was required to minimize the shock of losing familiar parent figures and acquiring new ones. We knew that familiar people, places and things decrease strangeness, and that breaking placement down into smaller pieces could make it more acceptable, but we were sure that even more important than these was the child's understanding of what was happening to him. It is hard to know how much a child understands before he can use words himself but he does have unspoken ways of letting us know even by six months of age, perhaps earlier in some children. We must not take the easy way out and simply say he is too young to understand. He is not. Experience in child placement has shown that a very young child can understand enough to enable him to accept the new parents and settle down with them. He can be helped to understand that he is going to a new Mummy and Daddy in a different house and that he will be taking his clothing, toys and anything like a favourite blanket along with him. He can understand that the old Mummy will miss him, but she still wants him to go. He can be helped to feel the confidence of the foster mother and worker in the plan. The tone of voice and the feelings behind the words are very important here, as these will be better understood than the words themselves. With older children it is not the *number* of get-acquainted visits, but the degree to which the child understands and feels he is participating that is important. It is frustrating to feel that things are being done *to* one by other people without even a chance to express one's feelings about it. The development of relationships cannot be forced and it is natural for a child to resist.

It is understandable that this may be upsetting to the foster mother or nursery staff or even to the caseworker, and they may favour a quick move to get it all over with at once, or a gradual move that makes the new parents familiar but still incomprehensible figures to the child. They hope to make it easy by avoiding tears and unpleasant scenes, but these methods leave the child's grief unexpressed, possibly to cause difficulties later. It is not so much the unfortunate experiences children have known as the repression of their feelings about these experiences, that often gives serious trouble later. So it is the child's understanding of placement, rather than the length of time between introduction and placement, that is important. A small child's conception of time is likely to be different from ours, and a few meetings very close together may be better preparation for a move than many meetings spread over a longer period. Yet there is need for flexibility in preparation and placement as each child is different. As one psychiatrist long associated with an adoption agency has said, 'Sensitive timing of the various stages of adoption attuned to the particular child's inner pace is a vital ingredient of reassurance; destructive anxiety can mount when certain steps of the process are too prolonged . . . however, panic may stem from feeling rushed and stampeded'.[9]

As might be expected, the Project staff handled some placements more skilfully than others and learned from experience. They always tried not to inject themselves too much into the situation, leaving the adopters free to decide whether to take the child and to express their feelings freely about him. We found it was very important that the workers who knew the adopters best should be present when the child was introduced and again when the adopters took him home. We felt increasingly that adopters should not be sent out to a nursery, foster home or mother-and-baby home alone for their first meeting with their baby, although this is the practice in some agencies. Adopters should be able to share their feelings about this baby with the adoption worker who has been concerned about their application from the beginning. Their reactions will be familiar to her and she can evaluate their reactions in this present situation much better than a different worker. The placement is an agency matter, too, and if the social worker is not present it may become a transaction between the adopters and the baby's caretaker. If it is desirable to withhold the adopters' name from the person caring for the baby this becomes very awkward for adopters visiting alone, but it can be handled easily by the person who knows them both.

The worker concerned with the child also will want to be present at this time, if possible, as this is reassuring to the foster mother or matron. The importance of this worker being present when the placement involves an older baby or toddler is obvious, because she can become a link between the child's past and future. She can gauge the child's reaction to the family and to this move, and can supplement

H

the caretaker's efforts to help the youngster understand and accept it. We usually suggested that adopters should not bring their other children on the first day of meeting the new baby because they would need to give all their attention to getting to know this child and also because we wanted them to be free to make their decision without the children entering into it. This is not a matter children can decide and they should not have the feeling of omnipotence toward the new child that this can bring, nor should the adopted child later feel his place in the family is held on sufferance of the older children. However, most adopters liked to bring their other children along on the day they came to take the baby home, thus making it a full family affair. This assumed the adopters were able to divide their attention sufficiently to provide the new baby with warmth and comforting, while at the same time giving the older children all the little attentions they were accustomed to, and answering their innumerable questions about the baby.

There is a good deal of discussion in this country about the advisability of natural parents and adopters meeting. For practical purposes this usually means the mother and the adopters, as few natural fathers have been involved to this extent. To our American and Canadian colleagues, confidentiality in adoption is thought to be one of the advantages of agency placements over direct or third-party placements, and the idea of the natural mother and adoptive parents meeting or being known to each other is the very thing they take elaborate precautions to avoid. However, the whole matter of confidentiality has been stressed rather less in British adoptions, and some people believe (as in Scotland) that the grown-up adopted child should be offered the information necessary for looking up his natural parents if he wants to do so. This is again different from North American agency adoptions where the relationship between natural parents and child is severed permanently, and the child becomes completely the child of the adopters, who have been chosen by the agency after the mother has legally relinquished the child and the agency has accepted custody. The British agency's role is more that of a go-between for the natural mother and the adopters. Which of these concepts is more acceptable to the natural parents and adopters is not known, because they are likely to comply with the traditions of their agency and no research has been done on this so far as we know.

The question of whether natural mothers and adopters should meet may be tied up with the whole philosophy of placement. What we do not want to do is put natural parents, child or adopters in a double bind. Is adoption a final and complete break between the child and his natural parents? Do we offer a natural mother the right to give up her child to new parents with the assurance of confidentiality, so that she can make a life for herself apart from him if she feels this is the best plan; or do we expect her to plan her life so that she can receive him back years later as a young adult if he wants to come, or even if he is just curious? Do we offer adopters a child they can make their own and to whom they can offer that kind of security, or are they expected to share him with the natural parents who decided to give him up? We know it is important for adopters to accept the fact that this child was born to someone else, but unless we place him with them with a full expectation that he will, nevertheless, become their child we are confusing adoption with another type of care – namely long-term fostering.

Follow-up studies with adults who were adopted as children have shown that most adopted children identify with their adopters and consider them as their real parents, even when they have been curious about the identity of their natural parents.[10] It seems to us that this should be our aim in adoption and that whatever methods are employed should serve this end. This brings us back to the question of the natural mother and adopters meeting. Will it help or hinder the natural mother in carrying through the plan she has decided is best, and in making a satisfactory life for herself apart from this child? Will it help or hinder the adoptive parents in making this child a full member of their family, a child who can grow up identified with them in a healthy way? We have heard two adoptive parents (not in the Project) say many years afterward, when their children were adolescents, that it would have been helpful to have met the mother, as they could then have described her better to the child. One adoptive couple in the Project said, in a group meeting some months after legal adoption, that they would have welcomed meeting the mother, as a description given by the agency had made them sure they would like her. Another adoptive mother said she often thinks she ought to let the mother see the child now and again to see what a lovely child he is. None of these people had asked to meet the mother, and the idea voiced from the vantage point of legal adoption seemed to be to reassure the mother that they were able to give the child good care. Saying it at this stage is quite different from wanting to meet the natural mother while it might still have been arranged, and before they had been able to prove themselves as adoptive parents. When asked in post-adoption discussion groups, only a few adopters said they wished they had met the mother. The others were adamant that they did not want to and felt it was better not to do so.

At least one agency has told us they ask all natural mothers and adopters if they wish to meet, and in fact encourage this so that a large proportion of them do so. Many other agencies do not raise this question and it is almost never proposed to them by a mother or by adopters. It seems as though this may be something in which clients follow in the way the agency leads, most of them doing whatever their social worker proposes. One Project adoptive mother, who already had a biological child, suggested meeting the natural mother of the adopted child, but that particular mother had returned home to Asia. Only one natural mother asked to meet her child's adoptive parents and this was not until two weeks after the child was placed. The father of one of the Project babies wanted a trusted older relative to see the child with the adopters (to be sure she was happy) some while after placement, and this was arranged in the adoption worker's office without the adopters and the relative actually meeting. Possibly the Project's emphasis on confidentiality, and an explanation of all that went into the assessment of children and adopters, may have conveyed to the others sufficient confidence in the suitability of the placement. Or as suggested above, perhaps the idea of meeting is something that does not occur to most natural parents and adopters coming to an agency unless the possibility is raised by the worker.

The one Project mother, who felt her future happiness depended upon meeting the adopters just once, would not have insisted if told it was impossible. This was an Asian mother and the adopters were English. The mother felt that she had let the child go into a vacuum and she needed to see that the adopters were real people, that they were not 'poor' and would give the child a good education. Several of her friends at the mother-and-baby home had met the people who were going to adopt their babies, and it seemed this made her feel remiss in not doing the same. She did not ask to see the baby again, just the adopters, and she offered to wait until after the legal adoption. The worker asked the mother to think it over and be quite sure she really wanted this, saying the Project would not stand in the way of a meeting after legal adoption if the adopters were willing. Shortly before the date of the court hearing the adopters were told in a home interview of the mother's wish, and a meeting was arranged for a week after the court hearing. Holding the meeting after the legal adoption made it acceptable to the adopters, as something they felt they could do for the sake of the mother. The meeting took place in the office of the caseworker who had worked with both mother and adopters. The worker introduced them without using names and stayed with them, the meeting lasting about ten minutes. Both parties had dressed rather specially for the occasion and were tense and nervous, but spoke graciously and warmly to each other. The mother had always wanted a photograph of the baby after placement and the adopters gave it to her at this time, and assured her that they loved the child as though she had always been theirs. Fortunately, the mother and adopters liked each other, and in talking with the worker very soon after the meeting they both expressed their satisfaction with it. The effects of such a meeting when the participants do not like or understand each other can only be imagined. At a group discussion some months later, this adoptive mother said it had been harder than she had anticipated, but she was not sorry they had met because now she would be able to tell the child that she looked eaxctly like her first mother. For a day or so after the meeting, the adoptive mother had been very upset and had felt the child was not really hers, but this feeling left her rather quickly. Whether telling the child she looks exactly like her natural mother will help the child to identify with her adoptive mother is questionable, but since the adoptive mother feels that she, too, resembles the baby, perhaps the child will be more able to see the two mothers as similar and to identify with them as one person.

The Project's experience with this meeting between adopters and natural mother, after an Adoption Order had been made, seemed to us quite different from meeting the mother on the day of placement or at the time of meeting the baby for the first time. For adopters – particularly those without other children – this day is the culmination of years of longing, so that coping with their own emotions would seem to make it hard for them to consider the mother's feelings as adequately as they would want to, and the sharp awareness of her loss would detract from the joy of their first moments with their child. Surely no social worker would expect a mother to bring her baby to adopters, meeting them for the first (and last) time when they are deciding whether to take the baby. What if they did not take the child, or would they feel under these circumstances any freedom to decide against taking him? The Project staff feels that any meeting between adopters and natural parents should be carefully planned and carried out as to timing and should be on neutral but familiar ground with the worker present. Such a planned meeting may strengthen an adoption, if both parties really want it or if it is essential to the future happiness of one of them. If this is their own wish, and an action taken on their own initiative, who are we to deny it? As social workers, we are committed to enabling people to be self directing so that they can live fuller lives. Too many rules and regulations built up out of our own anxiety may be restrictive if applied routinely. So perhaps it is best not to have a hard-and-fast rule about natural parents and adopters meeting or not meeting. Perhaps adoption workers should be guided by the meaning such a meeting can have for these two sets of parents, being aware that the intense feelings involved in such a confrontation give it potentialities for distress or for great satisfaction.

REFERENCES

(1) Seglow, Jean, *Introductory Paper on Adoption*, presented at Annual Conference of National Bureau for Co-operation in Child Care, Edinburgh, September 1968.

(2) Brenner, Ruth, *A Follow-up Study of Adoptive Families*, Child Adoption Research Committee, New York, 1951.

(3) *Child Welfare League of America Standards for Adoption Service* (revised), CWLA, New York 1968, p. 33.

(4) *ibid.*, p. 36.

(5) Rowe, Jane, *Parents, Children and Adoption*, Routledge & Kegan Paul, London, 1966, p. 221.

(6) Kirk, H. David, *Shared Fate*, Free Press, New York; Collier-Macmillan Ltd, London, 1964, p. 114.

(7) Yarrow, Leon, 'Separation from Parents in Early Childhood', *Review of Child Development Research* (Hoffman and Hoffman), Russell Sage Foundation, New York, 1964, p. 122.

(8) Charnley, Jean, *The Art of Child Placement*, University of Minnesota Press, Minneapolis (USA), 1955, p. 14.

(9) Bernard, Viola, 'Application of Psychoanalytic Concepts to Adoption Agency Practice', *Psychoanalysis and Social Work*, ed. by Marcel Hyman, International Universities Press, 1953.

(10) McWhinnie, Alexina M., *Adopted Children: How They Grow Up*, Routledge & Kegan Paul, London, 1967. Also, unpublished study by Lutheran Social Service of Minnesota (USA).

CHAPTER 7

THE PERIOD FROM PLACEMENT TO
LEGAL ADOPTION

Supervisory Visits

An agency that places a child with prospective adopters is required by law to 'make adequate arrangements for the supervision of the infant' until the adopters have given notice to their local authority of their intention to adopt him. The placing agency also is required to arrange that the child shall be visited within one month of placement 'and thereafter as often as the society's case committee deem necessary'.[1] When the adopters have notified their local authority, the child becomes a 'protected child', and a representative of the local authority children's department is required to visit him from time to time to satisfy himself as to the child's well being and 'give such advice as to his care and maintenance as may appear to be needed'.[2] These visits are commonly referred to as 'welfare supervision'.

When the prospective adopters are ready to proceed with the adoption, they submit an application to the court, but an Adoption Order cannot be made until the child has been in the care and possession of the adopters for at least three consecutive months immediately preceding the date of the Order, not counting any time before the child was six weeks old. Such an application to the court is followed by the court appointing a guardian *ad litem* (i.e. a guardian for the purpose of the adoption proceedings), to represent the child's interests by inquiring into all the circumstances of the placement, and by interviewing the adopters as well as the natural mother and often the putative father. The person who acts as guardian is nearly always a probation officer or a child care officer, and the report she writes is likely to be endorsed by the court.

Since a representative of the local authority will be visiting the home, and later the guardian *ad litem* will visit, too, some agencies do not feel any further visits by the placement agency are necessary, but the Project felt this post-adoption contact to be important and went well beyond the letter of the law in practice. Usually the Project worker visited the adoptive home within a week of placement, having already had a telephoned account of how the arrival home and the first night had gone. Visits were then made approximately monthly, but more often if any useful purpose could be served. There were three major reasons for remaining so closely in touch. The first was the belief that the social worker who had got to know the adopters over a period of months, and had discussed with them many of their feelings about becoming parents to this unknown baby, was probably the best person to be on hand once the baby had finally arrived. It was hoped that by that time adopters would feel they could talk freely to their worker about anything that concerned them regarding the baby, his natural parents, or their own feelings in their new role. Secondly, the worker was the link between the baby's past and present, and if there were further details about his past care or development that the new parents wanted to know it was hoped that she could supply them. Thirdly, the worker was also the link between the baby and his natural mother, or anybody else who had previously cared for him, and she wanted to be able to report back on how he was settling in. The worker wrote to the natural mother after making the first visit to the adoptive home, and made it clear to her that she would be visiting the baby until the legal adoption, and the mother could inquire of her how things were going if she wanted to. We always tried to ensure that the mothers were still in touch with their original workers (usually a moral welfare worker or a child care officer), but some mothers kept in close touch with us too. Most seemed relieved to know there was an intermediary between them and their child, and that the baby had not gone somewhere completely unknown.

Many foster parents, too, were glad to know that the worker they had met would continue to supervise the baby, and we always tried to let them know how the child settled. One foster couple, who had gone to great trouble in bringing the baby to London several times for the adopters to get to know him, said how much they appreciated being brought into the arrangements for him, and being kept informed afterwards of how he was settling; in their own words this was 'being treated as human beings, with feelings'. Often it seemed the babies they fostered were whisked away from their home by a social worker, who might well not be the one who would be supervising the child in his new home, and who was unable to give them any news of what happened to him after he had gone.

Although we felt it important to keep in close touch with the adoptive families, some of them told us later that they did not feel as free to use the casework help available as we had hoped. Even knowing the worker concerned apparently does not completely outweigh for adopters the feeling of being 'on probation', and the knowledge that if something goes wrong they could lose the child. One couple had serious doubts about one aspect of their child's physical development, but did not mention it to their worker until after the legal adoption had gone through, perhaps fearing that the order might not be granted, or that the child might be removed, especially as the Project had stated that its aim was to place only fully healthy babies. Since a case was known to them where a judge had refused to make a full adoption order until a medical query was cleared up, such a fear was perhaps not unfounded, although the Project itself would have been most unlikely to suggest the child's removal unless the adopters themselves had felt it was best.

Sometimes it happens that a couple does not realize the full implications of becoming parents until the child actually arrives. This is so with many natural parents too, but adopters may have had a much shorter period of preparation. Few of the Project adopters had a nine-month 'pregnancy' between acceptance and placement. Also the child may well be several months old when he comes to them. Suddenly to find oneself in sole charge of a strange infant can be a frightening experience, to say nothing of the adaptation to new emotions and changes in relationships involved in becoming adoptive parents.

The Project felt it important to be on hand to help and support adopters through this phase of adjustment. In addition the very small size of the Project meant that there was never a wide choice of suitable homes for any one child, so that when a baby was ready for placement, for whom we had what seemed the right home, we sometimes felt obliged to proceed with placement straightaway even if the timing was not entirely ideal from the adopters' point of view. One or two couples later told us the baby had come rather too quickly after their applications were accepted. For instance, the baby we placed with one childless couple was a rather advanced little girl of several months, and the adopters found it took time to get used to her ways and to the demands she made on them, as well as to their new roles as parents. Not expecting to have a baby so quickly, they found the first weeks a great strain, and at one time wondered if taking on a baby had been a mistake. The worker helped them to sort out their feelings, which revealed that their love for the baby and their desire to be parents were strong enough to outweigh their fatigue and concern over the physical care of a very active, precocious child. The worker was able to help them accept the validity of their mixed feelings and adjust to their new situation, which they finally did very satisfactorily.

The close contact maintained by the worker during the period before legal adoption could arouse varied reactions. One or two adopters later admitted they had thought the mother was changing her mind every time an appointment was made to visit, even though they had known the worker would be coming regularly. One or two felt they ought to be producing problems to discuss, to justify the visits, and almost felt guilty that everything was going well. On the whole, however, the families seemed glad of the continuing contact and support, and many expressed appreciation of it in the post-adoption discussion groups. It seemed to give them a greater sense of security to know they would be helped through the whole process of the adoption until it was legalized, and that their worker was always available to them if any worry or problem arose. The worker's attendance at the court with them seemed to be appreciated and, although it is said many agencies could not afford the time and expense involved, we did find it rounded off the whole experience for both adopters and worker.

One of the services the Project provided at this stage was obtaining application forms from the court, which were passed on partially completed to the adopters. When they had filled in the sections referring to themselves, they returned the forms to the Project where the details concerning the natural parents were added, and the application was then submitted directly to the court. It was done this way to spare the applicants having to know the full name and address of the natural mother (and the putative father if involved), which many said they did not want to know. A few even stopped the guardian from giving them this information later on. The mother did not have this information about them, as they were known to her only by a serial number, and they felt it best if neither knew the other's whereabouts.

From the adopters' point of view, the hardest thing about this period is the knowledge that the natural mother can change her mind and take the baby back. One would like the length of the supervision period to be more flexible, so that the adoption could be legalized when the child and family have grown together, whether this is accomplished in a few weeks or several months. Older children, especially, need longer to settle in, but the adopters' constant fear of the natural mother withdrawing her consent makes it impractical to prolong supervision beyond the legal minimum. Even though the Project adopters knew that the mother had signed her consent to this adoption before the child was placed, they were fully aware that this could be used as proof of her decision *only if she had not changed her mind*. Does this suggest that the 'consent' is virtually meaningless? Admittedly, once the adoption application has been lodged, the mother cannot withdraw her child without explaining her reasons to the court and obtaining a decision in her favour, but as one of the Project families found to their cost, this affords the adopters little protection.

Two couples in the Project had the unhappy experience of having to part with a child when the natural mother changed her mind. In the first case, an unusually high risk was taken with the full knowledge of the adopters and the Project team, since adoption seemed to offer the only real security for the child's future. This mother changed her mind a few days after placement. In the second instance, the mother had nobody to help her with her conflicts, and it was not until she received notification of the hearing that she indicated her change of mind. This was a bitter blow to the adopters, who had become devoted to the child, and they expressed very poignantly their feelings that it was almost worse to lose a child into an unknown future, as they were doing, than to lose a child by death. The case went to court, since the mother's notification of withdrawal of consent came within only a week of the hearing. The judge made the interesting comment that if the law enabled him to put the child's interests first, he would tend to sign the Order, but what the law required of him was to decide whether the mother was withholding her consent 'unreasonably'. Since he could not say she was, he felt obliged to decide that the child must return to her mother.

The loss of these babies caused great grief to both families, and it was clear that, even though both went on to adopt another child, the second one in no way replaced the first, who remained an individual in their memory. Particularly noreworthy was the effect of the loss on the older children in the family, for whom it was a very disturbing experience. It is hard enough to explain to a child about adoption, and why a mother may have to part with her baby, but how does one then explain why the baby is going back? And how does one help the child not to feel that he, too, may have to go away? Both couples reported a noticeable difference in the reactions of these children to the baby we later placed with them. The children found it hard to believe that the new child would remain with them, and one of them became very upset when a child care officer visited, as she feared the officer was going to take the baby away.

Experience with 'Welfare Supervision' and the Guardian ad litem
Fortunately, reclaims after adoption placement happen in only a very small minority of cases (2 per cent of voluntary agency placements in 1966). Yet the waiting period between placement and legal adoption is a very trying time, and adopters are in a particularly vulnerable position. They are caring for and coming to love a child as their own, but they know he is not yet their own, and they feel very much on trial as no other parents do. For instance, one mother said she had not dared to argue with a remark made by a health visitor, for fear of getting 'an adverse report'. The white adopters in the Project had the additional strain of getting used to doing something rather unusual in taking a child of different race into their family. They had to learn how to react to hostility, criticism or, at the least, surprise from the community, and sometimes even from the officials who visited them, such as one health visitor who asked sympathetically, 'Oh, couldn't you get a white child?'

In spite of the strains, most of our adopters felt fully committed to the child right from the start, and having got him they were anxious to begin the legal proceedings as soon as possible. Many of them notified the local authority the very next day, and the Project always immediately sent the children's department concerned a full report on the placement. The guardian *ad litem* would require a report from the placing agency, and it seemed logical to send it early, so the supervising officer could have the relevant background information before visiting.

The experiences of the Project families during this period raised a good many questions as to the purpose and value of 'welfare supervision', and its effect on adopters, as well as of its place in the overall work of a children's department. In some cases the supervising child care officer arrived at the adopters' house with a series of forms to complete regarding such facts as the number of rooms in the house and how long the couple had been married, all of which was in our report, but which the adopters had to go into all over again. On the other hand, when a child care officer had no such factual material to gather, she often seemed very unclear of her function and did little more than 'have a cup of tea and a chat, and admire the baby'. One officer never even saw the baby, as he was asleep each time she visited, and she said she would not disturb him.

It seems clear that there is an urgent need to clarify the exact purpose of the visits made to adopters, as well as to define the tasks of the various workers involved. How far does 'advice as to (the child's) care and maintenance' extend, for instance? One child care officer providing welfare supervision seemed to think it gave her the right (unasked) to advise an adoptive couple of different racial backgrounds to bring up the child in the Church of England, although the natural mother had not specified any religion for the child, and the adopters had made a very thoughtful decision to bring him up a Muslim, like his adoptive father. The child care officer then suggested that perhaps the boy could be a Muslim until he was five, and then change to the Church of England so as to fit in better at school! The appropriateness of the welfare supervisor advising parents about their child's religious upbringing was questionable, but the travesty of religious belief, which such a suggestion implied, was not likely to inspire confidence in a couple who apparently had given considerably more thought to the whole question than this adviser had.

The question of timing of visits is also one that needs to be examined. The child care officers sometimes made appointments for the first visit but rarely for any subsequent ones, so that the adopters tended to feel they were being 'checked up on' by surprise calls, even though some of them felt this was right, and that it might be the only way to ensure seeing them as they really were. Some departments insisted that the first visit must be the one to be made without an appointment, and in one case this resulted in no visit being made for ten weeks, as the child care officer always came when the adoptive mother was out. After the officer had left a card four or five times, the mother began to feel very guilty, but although she telephoned to offer to make an appointment, she was told the visit must be unannounced. She was left hoping the child care officer was in the area anyway, and not wasting too much time on all these abortive calls. Similar if less extreme experiences were mentioned by several adopters.

Another effect of not making appointments resulted in at least one of the adopters receiving three visits on the same day. The Project worker called by appointment, and the health visitor and child care officer both came in close succession, unannounced. This was not only wearing, but also time consuming and inconvenient for the adoptive mother, yet she felt helpless in the situation. A number of adopters mentioned how inconveniently timed the welfare visits had sometimes been. For example, to be seen at about 7 p.m. coming home with four weary young children after a day's outing and having to discuss adoption with a stranger while preoccupied with wanting to get a meal and put the baby to bed, seemed to one mother not the only or even the best way of assessing her ability for adoptive parenthood. No natural parent has to prove herself in quite so demanding a way, or feel at risk of having her child taken away from her if she lets her tiredness or harassment show too obviously.

The couples mostly found the child care officers friendly and pleasant, but in many instances commented on their extreme youth. One reported that the child care officer had expressed gratitude for being accepted by the adoptive mother in spite of her youthful appearance, as people often said she looked too young to know anything about such work. Several of the adopters said they thought their child care officer was rather inexperienced, and one suggested that, in a busy children's department, adoption duties probably ranked as a low priority and the 'most expendable' (i.e. the newest and youngest) member of staff was assigned to them. If the purpose of welfare supervision is merely to make sure that the child is being physically well cared for, perhaps it does not matter if adopters have this impression. They will accept that a young or inexperienced officer can carry out such a duty satisfactorily, although if this is all the supervision is, they may feel that the health visitor is already doing it. But, if the supervision involves a much deeper investigation of the whole adoptive situation and if, as happened in three-quarters of the Project cases, the same child care officer acts both as welfare supervisor and guardian *ad litem*, then it does seem unfortunate that the person bearing this heavy responsibility should appear so young and inexperienced. Adopters realize that the report presented by the guardian to the court is very important to the final decision, and they need to have confidence in the person who makes the report. If the child care officer seems lacking in confidence or unprofessional in her approach, this is bound to have an effect on the adopters, and it cannot be an easy task for the child care officer in these circumstances, either.

When different officers acted as welfare supervisor and as guardian *ad litem*, it was not always easy for the adopters to understand their separate functions. Often the same questions were asked by both, even though they perhaps came from the same children's department. The welfare supervisor might visit as often as every three weeks, but 'only for a chat', whereas the guardian might make a report to the court on the basis of only one visit. The adopters felt happier if they thought the guardian had really had the chance to get to know them, so they found it logical and less confusing if she had visited throughout the waiting period in the role of welfare supervisor, assuming the additional task of court representative once they had filed their application. This combination of roles also eliminated one extra person for the adopters to be 'inspected by', because there is no doubt that this is how the official visits are seen, no matter how considerate and helpful the workers may be. More than one adoptive mother told us that, however friendly their child care officer, they could not admit any worries to her lest she thought the adoption was not going well. In spite of this, many of them felt it was right for the child's well being to be safeguarded by an independent official, though more so in third-party or direct placements, where there is no other contact with a social worker at all. However, they felt that this would be possible without the multifarious visits of the welfare supervisor, the adoption agency worker, the health visitor, the guardian *ad litem* and possibly others. The representative of one local education department even called to tell a couple they would have to enter their infant for the primary school immediately as there might be no vacancies in five years time.

Many of our adopters felt that officers' time was being wasted in these duplicated visits covering ground already covered by the family study or by the Project's supervision. It was suggested that the statutory supervision might be linked to the adequacy of what is done by the placement agency. This may be hard for a children's department to assess, but it was clear that some of the officers concerned did make this kind of assessment; for instance, several child care officers said that because of the fullness of the Project's report they could see that intensive work had been done, and they would not need to visit very often themselves. Perhaps children's departments could make a practice of requiring detailed reports from adoption agencies *at the time of placement*, and assessing from these the need for additional visiting.

Experience with Adoption Hearings
Four of the Project's cases were heard in juvenile courts, the rest in county courts. The worker concerned usually consulted the local

children's department and most of them suggested the county courts. In one or two cases, it was indicated that a judge was known not to favour mixed-race adoptions, so the juvenile court was recommended, but mostly it was felt that the county court offered a chance of an earlier hearing, as well as greater legal competence in case of any difficulties. The adopters tended to share this feeling, and also usually preferred to go before a judge who would be unlikely to know them in other capacities, as local magistrates might. The Project worker concerned always tried to attend the hearing with the applicants. In all four of the juvenile court cases the applicants were put on oath, but this rarely happened in the county courts. The juvenile court hearings tended to be longer, varying between ten and thirty minutes, while the average county court hearing was four minutes (five of them lasting one minute or less, ten about two minutes). The couple whose hearing lasted thirty minutes felt it had been a 'long drawn out rigma-role' during which all the facts in the guardian's report had to be verified by them on oath. Another couple was very upset by the magistrates' requesting their older child to wait outside, when she had been carefully prepared for the occasion and knew what was happening. The adopters had felt this was very much a family affair, and particularly did not want the older child to feel excluded. Although the right to be present at a hearing is strictly limited, in most of our cases the older children in the family had been allowed to be present.

In either type of court, the setting was seldom very satisfactory. Adoption hearings are normally held in the magistrates' or judge's rooms before the main business of the court begins. Frequently there is no waiting room other than the main court room, where as often as not people are already arriving for later cases. Some clerks go to a good deal of trouble to keep adopters apart, and are discreet in calling them when it is their turn, but others let all comers mingle together and call out the names of the adopters for all to hear, thus doing away with all pretence at confidentiality. More than one couple thought that a woman of foreign appearance sitting nearby might be the natural mother come to have a look at her baby's new parents, and although it never was the mother, the woman concerned could certainly have heard the name of the adopters if she had wanted to. If new family courts are set up, they will be the logical place for adoptions to be heard, and it is hoped that arrangements will be such that they can be kept quite separate from other less pleasant proceedings.

On the other hand, the hearings in either court tended to be such an anti-climax that some adopters wondered why they need appear at all. In one case the judge had signed the Order before coming into the room; he merely told them so, and wished them well. In the absence of any set procedure, many judges seemed uncertain how to make the couples feel it was worth having come. Some reminded the applicants that the child they were adopting would become as much theirs as if born to them, and a number stressed the additional importance of telling the child he was adopted, but others just talked to the children, or inquired about the father's interests, or chatted about something they had in common.

In at least eight of the hearings, the judge inquired what kind of religious upbringing the child would have. These questions seemed to be unrelated to the natural mother having specified a religion for the child. When the adopters had no religious affiliation, they said they would not be giving the child any denominational teaching, but would allow him to decide for himself when older. In more than one instance the judge seemed perturbed by this, and spoke of the possible handicap to a child of being brought up in a nominally Christian country with religious teaching at school, but without instruction at home. One judge looked at the baby girl and said, 'I understand religion a is great comfort, especially to women'. Another requested an assurance that at least the adopters would not actively try to turn the child against religion. Adopters felt at a disadvantage because they wanted to defend their views, but were afraid to antagonize the judge in whose hands lay the decision regarding the child. Several of them said later that they felt the matter of religious upbringing was outside the judge's jurisdiction, and that his personal views on the subject were no more valid than their own and considerably less relevant.

Some judges commented on the fact of the child's being coloured (one asked if the adopters were aware he was!) and, while none expressed active disapproval, one or two seemed a little perplexed as to why a couple should want to adopt a child of another race. One said, 'I salute your broadmindedness', and several congratulated the adopters on the public service or the 'wonderful thing' they were doing. Actually, whatever part might have been played by broadmindedness or other such attributes in the decision to adopt had long since been outweighed by more natural parental feelings towards the child, but the adopters took such comments as they were meant, appreciating that the judge was trying to make them feel comfortable. Above all, they were relieved when the Order was signed, and felt they would

I

not have minded what had been said so long as the adoption was legalized.

The judge has a difficult task in an adoption hearing. All the work has been done; he has usually made his decision when studying the reports beforehand, and there is little left to say. Yet for the adopters it is the climax of a long period of waiting. Perhaps a short form of ceremony might be drawn up for adoptions, as for civil marriages. There would then be a given moment at which the child would become legally a member of his new family, the participants would have something to remember, and the judge would be spared having to make conversation in order to make the proceedings relaxed and agreeable.

Whenever this was discussed at group meetings, most of the adopters felt something specific was needed to give a sense of occasion. Those with older children nearly all felt that attending a hearing gave the children something to remember, and was a help in explaining about adoption. A few adopters suggested they would be happy to have the legal formalities accomplished without any court appearance, as in Scotland.[3]

REFERENCES

(1) Adoption Act 1958, Sec. 34 (Part III).
(2) *ibid.*, Sec. 38 (Part IV).
(3) For a discussion of adoption practice in Scotland, see Triseliotis, John, 'Courts and Adoption Practice', *Case Conference*, Vol. 15, No. 5, September 1968.

CHAPTER 8

POST-ADOPTION DISCUSSION GROUPS

Purpose of the Groups

'Adjustment to adoption does not stop magically at the time of the adoption decree when agency contact usually terminates.'[1] Yet over the years it has been assumed that adoptive parents want to forget the agency after legal adoption, and the fact that so few have returned to seek advice or help from the adoption agencies has strengthened this view.

More recently some adoption workers have felt dissatisfied with discussions that can only be theoretical when the application is being studied, and have been worried by the inability of families to accept help during the supervision period with problems likely to arise later on. As we have seen, the period between placement and the granting of an Adoption Order is an anxious time for adoptive parents and they cannot think much beyond the impending court hearing. Afterwards, when the child has become legally theirs, they often begin to wish for help with the problems inherent in adoptive parenthood.

Iris Goodacre interviewed ninety couples who lived in one English county, and who had adopted a child two to five years earlier. She found that they had not even been very sure about the purpose of the 'supervision' they had received and that they hesitated to *seek* advice after the legal adoption. Yet they were very receptive to an opportunity for discussion and were curious about how other adopters had fared, whether they were encountering any special problems and how these were being dealt with.[2] Gochros' American study found marked disagreement between caseworkers and adoptive parents concerning the function of the post-placement period of supervision. The caseworkers saw themselves as helping in integrating the adoptive family, but the adopters saw them primarily as uninvited but benevolent authority figures. These parents, too, did not feel it appropriate to seek help from the agency for any problem arising after legal adoption, but they were definitely interested in agency sponsored discussion groups.[3]

A review of the literature, along with some inquiries, disclosed that several agencies in North America, and more recently one in Scotland, had held meetings for adoptive parents, and had found adopters responsive to the idea of helping each other through discussion. During the two years while our meetings were going forward, the idea of post-adoption discussion groups caught on and they are now being tried by quite a large number of agencies. The groups known to us earlier had been held from three years to fourteen or fifteen years after adoption. We wondered if discussion groups might be helpful as early as a few months after legal adoption, while the relationship with the agency was still intact. It seemed likely that such groups could be educational for adopters and at the same time yield some information on how they felt about many things. We thought the emphasis should be educational, with feelings and attitudes being explored on a conscious level. If a problem serious enough to require therapy should arise a plan could be made for securing the appropriate treatment.

When the possibility of holding discussion groups before the end of the Project was mentioned at pre-application meetings, the idea met with an enthusiastic response; later on during the adoption process couples sometimes inquired about whether such groups actually would be held. They quite often asked whether certain people they remembered from the pre-application meeting had taken a child, and there seemed to be real interest not only in continuing contact with the Project but also in some further meeting with other Project adopters. They were particularly keen to make their experience helpful to other adoptive parents directly, and also to help them indirectly by enabling the staff to learn from them something that could be applied to adoption practice generally, and especially to the placement of non-white children.

We wanted to experiment with post-adoption discussion groups to find out how to make them most acceptable and useful to these families. For example, could they benefit within three or four months after legal adoption, or does it take longer for questions and problems to present themselves? Would a series of three meetings held fortnightly or monthly be more acceptable and helpful than a more widely spaced series? How much structure in a meeting would produce the most fruitful discussion? Would meetings be more productive when couples had built-in problems in common, such as biological childlessness, several natural-born children as well as the adopted child, or residence in a racially homogeneous (or heterogeneous) community?

We believed that adoptive parents might have certain interests and concerns that they would like to discuss with each other and the agency if an opportunity were presented, and that social workers as well as adopters might have much to learn from such discussions. We felt that the Project presented a unique opportunity to take this assumption one step further and apply it to interracial adoption. Perhaps something could be learned about the attitudes and feelings of these parents toward their experience in adopting a non-white child, their present satisfactions and problems, and some of their anxieties about the future. These general subjects were broken down into smaller topics which we anticipated adopters might want to discuss, and which also would be of interest to the Project.

Topics of Interest and Value to Both Adopters and Staff
The past

I. The adopters' attitudes now towards the whole process of application, placement and supervision as employed in the Project, including their positive and negative criticism of the following.

A. The pre-application group meeting
   (i) as a method of screening inquiries
   (ii) as a method of learning about adoption in general and about the Project in particular

B. The family study as they experienced it, in regard to
   (i) timing – in general
   (ii) interviewing methods
   (iii) required medical information
   (iv) contacts with relatives and referees
   (v) timing of acceptance of application in relation to placement
   (vi) changes in their concept of the term 'family study', or 'investigation for adoption' since experiencing it

C. The placement process as they experienced it, including
   (i) the Project's method of giving them information about the child and his biological family

(ii) adequacy of the information given them on which *to make a decision* about taking this child

(iii) meeting the child for the first time

(iv) whether they ever wish they had met the child's natural mother or father

(v) getting to know the child

(vi) taking the child

D. 'Supervision' by the Project during the period between placement of the child and the granting of an Adoption Order

(i) length of time involved

(ii) number of visits

(iii) helpful or unhelpful aspects

(iv) adopters' concept of the role of the Project caseworker during this time

II. The adopters' feelings and attitudes towards statutory investigation and supervision after placement of the child in the family, including

A. 'Welfare supervision' by the children's department of their local authority

B. The work of the guardian *ad litem*

III. The adopters' feelings and attitudes toward their experience with the legal process, including

A. The Adoption Act

B. The court procedures

IV. What the adopters see as the most difficult experience they have had thus far in relation to adopting this child

The present

V. What adopters see as their present satisfactions and pleasures in adoption

VI. What adopters see as their present (or recent) problems in adoption

VII. The present attitude of grandparents, other relatives, friends and neighbours

A. Is this very different from their attitudes at time of application?

B. How much do race and colour enter into their attitudes now?

The future

VIII. The adopters' feelings now (some months after legal adoption) about telling the child he is adopted and that he once had other parents

    A. Whether they still expect to tell him of his adopted status

    B. When and how they plan to do this

    C. What obstacles they see to telling him

    D. Do they think the type and amount of information given them about the child and his background will facilitate 'telling' or make it even more of a problem?

    E. Whether they feel this will help or hinder them in telling the child he is adopted and in answering his questions about his origins

    F. What they most dread telling him

    G. How the fact of the child's racial difference enters into the problem of telling

IX. Whether anxiety about the child's future is a problem to adopters at this time, in relation to

    A. Entrance into the larger community as a school boy or girl

    B. Adolescent social activities

    C. 'Going steady'

    D. Employment

    E. Possible problems created for other children in the family during adolescence by the presence of an adopted brother or sister of different race

Method and Structure

As caseworkers, our expertise in helping was in the use of a one-to-one relationship, so we had to feel our way in working with the adopters in groups. If we had had training in social group work in addition to our experience with interracial adoption in the Project, we might have recognized and taken advantage of every opportunity the groups offered to make them more consistently meaningful. As it was, leaders were sometimes too active or too directive, setting their sights upon covering certain of the topics in the list just above. At other times a leader needed to be more directive in order to get the discussion beyond a superficial level or to see that a subject was not dropped on an unhelpful note. Occasionally, when someone was trying to make a point that obviously was not clear to the others, and they were getting nowhere with it, the leader had to try to express the thought in different words, sometimes as a generalization, other times by citing an example as an illustration. Some meetings continued beyond the allotted time and ended in an unfinished, ragged way. Some groups found it hard to pick up where they had left off at the previous meeting, and it helped both meetings when a leader summed up briefly at the end of one meeting and then recalled this to the group in just a very few words at the beginning of the next meeting.

As we approached the end of the Project, leaders felt some pressure to get certain information, with the result that they became much more directive, sometimes announcing at the beginning of a meeting that the adopters were free to discuss anything of interest to them, but that first the leader would suggest two or three specific topics on which the Project would like their views. When topics were announced thus at the start of a meeting, the whole session tended to be taken up with them and it became a little more like a question and answer session with very little spontaneity. On the other hand, when the invitations to the second or third meeting of a group encouraged them to suggest subjects for discussion, the subjects turned out to be of general interest and the persons raising them for discussion had already given them a good deal of thought and wanted to test their ideas by putting them to the group. This procedure led to particularly thoughtful discussions about such subjects as competition between a natural-born and an adopted child in a family; how much stress to put on the child's difference in colour; whether any attempt should be made to prepare a child for discrimination he may meet at some time in the future.

It had been decided in advance that the meetings would be small and as unstructured as possible, keeping in mind our goal that they should be useful to both the adopters and the staff. The same social worker would lead all the meetings in a particular series and a second worker would attend and act as Recorder. The same group of adoptive parents would be invited to all the meetings in a series, and the meetings would be held in the evening or on Saturday afternoon in a large room at the Project office, where tea or coffee could be served at the start. Meetings would be limited to six, seven or eight couples who could sit around a large square table facing one another. In practice, we found it best not to add any new members to a group after the first meeting, because they were not easily or quickly accepted and their presence tended to slow down the discussion and keep it at a superficial level. No one accepted the offer to remain anonymous,[4] and no one objected to the use of a tape recorder at some of the meetings.

Eight series of meetings were held involving a total of fifty couples, and there were from two to four meetings in each series. Three meetings held about a month apart seemed to be the most satisfactory. Every couple was included except one who had returned to an assignment overseas. Not everyone attended every meeting in his series, but in most cases the absence seemed to be unavoidable. As some of these families lived as far as fifty miles from London and had several young children to be cared for, we felt the very good attendance confirmed their earlier interest in meeting with other adopters and in contributing their experience to the Project's findings.

We were not able to experiment with the composition of groups as much as we had wished, since groups had to be made up of those couples whose Adoption Orders had been made at approximately the same time in order to include everyone before the end of the Project. Some of the people in the first group had had their adopted child for well over a year, but in succeeding groups some adopters had had their child for only six or seven months. Although this was not ideal, it did seem that they were able to make good use of the discussions even then.

Fortunately, just by taking the adopters in this order we found that the composition of all the groups was not the same as to race, socio-economic status and number of children. Two groups were made up entirely of couples with mixed families of natural born and adopted children. Unfortunately, there was no group composed entirely of couples who had only the adopted child. One may theorize that this is the reason there was no discussion about the feelings that had been associated with unsuccessful efforts to have a natural-born child, which is a subject known to trouble many such people long after they have become parents through adoption.

One group was made up entirely of English couples, mostly university graduates. Two others were composed of English people who might roughly be classified as middle class and upper working class. The other groups were interracial (one essentially working class, another essentially middle class and three mixed). Something could be said for and against each of these groupings. Whatever their background, these people all shared a common interest and a common aspiration in their wish to be good adoptive parents to a non-European child. One felt the English adopters in mixed groups learned just a little about what it feels like to be coloured, and the adopters of other races came to appreciate the added problems of those who had adopted a child of different race. Getting to know each other seemed to be an enriching experience for both.

It was impossible to set up groups on the basis of the area in which people lived, because of the Project's small numbers and limited time span, but several people, who said they would like more such discussions in the years ahead, suggested organizing them on a regional basis. In addition to making it easier to attend meetings, some people thought there might be an advantage in keeping in touch with one another, and that this was more likely if they lived in the same county or on the same side of London.

It was planned that the first meeting in each series would be largely unstructured and exploratory, in order (1) to encourage the adopters to get acquainted and to feel comfortable enough with one another to risk expressing their real feelings, and (2) to learn how these particular adopters would like to use these meetings. Later meetings would be semi-structured, taking into consideration the suggestions the group had made in the first meeting and teaming these up, if possible, with related topics in the list that the Project had rather hoped they might want to discuss. As already mentioned, this plan was adhered to more strictly with some groups than with others. If meetings were being planned entirely for the benefit of adopters, without the secondary need to compile information, the meetings could be even more unstructured, so that each group could pursue its own interests.

Experience with the Groups
The adopters very soon found they had much in common, and they almost as quickly began to share with one another their problems and pleasures as adoptive parents. As adopters, and particularly as inter-racial adopters, they realized they constituted a minority group, and their awareness of this made them welcome the support of others in the same situation. As two or three people said, 'Taking a child of another race shows you who your friends really are'. Another father said, 'It is interesting to know those who are in this with you'.

Some of the non-white families were surprised that English people felt so warmly toward these children that they had chosen to adopt one into their family. This led some of the non-European adopters to discuss the problems of a coloured child growing up in an English family and to consider whether non-Europeans should be urged to adopt these children; it was agreed that a child needs parents who really want him, whatever thier race, but there are certain advantages for a child in growing up with parents of his own race and colour.

As might be expected, members of every group were concerned about how, when and what to tell the child about adoption and the natural parents who gave him up. This came up spontaneously in every group. A good deal had been said to adopters before and after placement about 'telling'. This had been explained as a gradual sharing of the meaning of adoption with a youngster from early childhood to adolescence, but adoptive parents had found it difficult to assimilate this before the child was legally theirs. Where the physical appearance of the child was markedly different, there was no temptation to withhold the fact of adoption, since it was so obvious, but even there the timing and approach to telling were matters of concern.

One non-European couple, whose baby was very like the adoptive father in appearance, found strength in the group's certainty that he must be told. This couple found the meetings a place to exchange ideas about adoption as a method of having a family, and they came to accept that their son once had other parents, and some day he might even be interested in them, yet this need not mean the end of the world or even a serious threat to their family life.

It was very generally believed that a child should be told of his adoption early, certainly before he goes to school. There was agreement about the desirability of creating an atmosphere of freedom in the home, which would be conducive to a child asking the questions that were in his mind with the assurance of a truthful answer. Everyone felt this should be so in regard to the giving of sex information, but that it was particularly important in the relationship between an adopted child and his parents, because telling about adoption was not something that could be done once and for all. It would come up from time to time with the child's increasing understanding, and if the child did not mention it, adopters had a responsibility to bring the subject into the open, as some children hesitate to ask something that may upset their parents. The idea, that resistance to 'telling' might be associated with some residue of their earlier rejection of adoption as a means of having or increasing their family, was something they had not considered, but it seemed to strike a responsive chord when it was suggested by the staff. Most people felt the word 'adopted' should not be used every time a child was introduced, especially beyond babyhood, as this tended to emphasize the feeling of difference and might cause a child to think the parents did not want anyone to mistake him for their 'own'. Most people felt the best support they could give to the child would be to say 'He is ours', rather than to explain his different physical appearance by saying the child had a non-European parent.

One group was interested in an African member's comments about the duties of children toward their parents in his culture, which led him to think that an adopted child might feel some loyalty to his natural mother. As this loyalty was associated with religion, it led to a spirited disagreement between two English parents about the place of religion in setting standards of conduct, particularly in regard to what should be expected of the parent-child relationship.

One couple felt so pleased about their child's good background that they did not care who knew about it, but the general feeling was that the details of the background belong to the child and should be told only to him – with the exception of medical details which should be given to the family doctor.

With English adopters it was not a question of whether a child should be told, but when, how and what to tell him. When would he first notice that he looked different from the family? How should this be explained? One mother said she would just say, 'God made you brown.' Others planned to say that people come in different colours. It was felt that a child might recognize his different appearance before he was old enough to link this with adoption. Only one child was old enough to be aware of colour and he had been two years old at placement and knew about having his family by adoption. His adoptive mother thought he preferred Asians and identified with them, since he showed a particular fondness for an Asian friend of the family. Another English mother had tried to tell her not-quite-three-year old Asian daughter about being 'brown' and adopted, but the child insisted, 'I'm not brown, you're brown', and showed great dislike of an Asian woman who visited the house.

One West Indian adoptive mother warned her group against over-emphasizing the child's difference. She said the West Indian adolescents that she knew, who were growing up in Britain, were refusing to accept the label 'coloured'; they would not think of themselves as different and found it very objectionable to be reminded of it. She said that she herself had been made more aware of her colour by the discussions at these meetings, that she usually did not think of herself as different from the English people she worked with every day. Although no one else expressed this quite so well, it may have been the feeling behind the idea held by most of the non-white adopters that the treatment these children might expect from other children and adults in the community was much the same as for any child. They suggested that all babies and young children attract the attention of strangers; children with red hair or freckles, youngsters who are overwieght, etc., are called unpleasant names by other children just as non-European children may be called names referring to their colour. One African adoptive father felt this way about his natural-born child who is sometimes referred to by his school mates as 'Blackie'. He handled this with the boy by pointing out that unpleasant things happen to all, whether black or white. This child's English mother felt he might be more upset by name-calling than he showed, as he always wanted to be white except when in a group of Africans. Both white and non-white adopters felt they must help a child to accept his racial identity, but they did not think this would be easy.

There was conflict in the minds of some of the English adopters as to how much the Asian, African or West Indian cultural heritage should be emphasized. Would a child being raised in an English family be as English as anyone, or would he have a special interest in the culture of a faraway land in Asia, Africa or the Caribbean? It was suggested by someone that it was the adopters themselves who probably were most interested in this. Some felt that teaching a child pride in his race would help him to withstand discrimination. These people felt they should learn all they could about the country from which their child's first parents had come, and should give the child opportunities to meet people from that culture. Other parents felt this was stressing the difference and that they could only bring up the child as English. One adoptive mother said, 'We have a little English girl in a brown skin'. Another said, as the children were growing up in the British culture, why make any difference in this just because of their appearance?

Concern about culture led into a discussion of the relative influence of heredity and environment. This came up in nearly every group as a subject many people felt confused about, especially about whether there really are any racially inherited characteristics such as laziness, gentleness, aggression or cheerfulness. These discussions disclosed more concern about heredity and background than had been acknowledged during the family studies, when the adopters' interest had been focused upon getting a child. Now they were faced with the problem of how to explain the biological parents and their reasons for giving up the child, in such a way that he would be able to integrate his two sets of parents and not be in conflict between them.

Some people felt they would like to know more about the child's background in order to know what to expect, but many more felt they only wanted to know a few things about the natural parents, and these they had been given. Some people felt that learning all might include something worrying that they could do nothing about, and others thought detailed information about the child's first parents might stand between the child and his adopters making their acceptance of each other in a permanent parent-child relationship more difficult.

The adopters related some incidents from their experience which showed the confusion the public feels about heredity. One adoptive mother was asked in all seriousness, 'Do you have to cook all his food with curry?', and another was asked when the baby was just learning to talk, 'Is that an Indian accent?' A baby clinic was said to show pleased surprise that the English adoptive mother was not feeding an Asian baby foreign foods.

There had been some minor incidents of unpleasantness and hurt because of the child's colour (perhaps forerunners of more serious incidents when he is older?) but most of the adopters had taken these in their stride, charging them to ignorance, idle curiosity or inability to change with the times. Most groups welcomed the moral support of sharing these experiences with one another. In an interracial working-class group, the telling of some rather unpleasant incidents was relieved by some good-humoured comments and the opportunity to laugh at oneself in an atmosphere of solidarity and goodwill.

Sometimes it was relatives, other times total strangers or health or welfare officials who reacted negatively or thoughtlessly to the presence of a non-white child in an English family. Almost without exception the child attracted an unusual amount of attention from strangers. Most often they admired the baby and made a fuss over him or said, 'How wonderful of you to take him,' but occasionally remarks were overheard suggesting criticism of a white mother and a coloured child. As one woman said, 'Everyone has a question in their mind when they see you with a coloured child'. In another case, someone put the thought into words saying, 'That is not your husband's child'. Another adoptive mother was in a supermarket with her two young children and the adopted baby, when an elderly man asked if she had adopted the baby, then wanted to know why, and went on to say in a loud and excited voice, 'All these types coming into the country are a menace to society, and like the Irish, are likely to murder us all in our beds'. The mother wisely did not reply, but the verbal attack left her shaking and angry. Another adopter said, 'One needs heaps of confidence to reject all this undermining criticism'. Apparently, foster mothers need this confidence, too, because another adoptive mother was mistaken for a foster mother by a woman in the park, who interfered when she would not buy the child an ice-cream by saying accusingly, 'Poor little chap – I know what you people are – you do it just for the money!'

An adoptive father, telephoning to book a caravan holiday, was asked the size of his family. Learning it was a family of seven, the voice on the other end of the telephone said, 'You aren't coloured, are you?' Upon being told that one of the children was coloured, the booking clerk said, 'Oh we don't mind about the children'.

Nearly all the white families had encountered ignorant questions or well-meaning curiosity from neighbours, acquaintances or strangers, but only two or three families had had any real trouble with their close relatives after a child was in the home, though several others had to handle the idea of interracial adoption with them in advance. Several adopters reported that grandparents had found the child more lovable than they had expected and they had accepted him wholeheartedly, but one grandmother was said to be Victorian, and her son believed she would never accept the adoption except 'on the surface'. One is naturally apprehensive about the future where an adoptive mother says her sister 'can't stand coloured people' but is devoted to this child. Another grandmother, who had never accepted her daughter's marriage to a man of different race and religion, had never seen the adopted child or shown the slightest interest in her. However, the two families had been estranged for several years and the adoptive mother believed the rejection of a natural-born child of this union would have been even greater. One English family had endured a family party at which a sister and brother-in-law had not spoken to them and then had planned a family photograph omitting the adopted child. Granny saved the day by refusing to have her picture taken without *all* her grandchildren included, but two years passed before the sister and her husband finally accepted the child into the extended family.

We found most of the middle-class adopters more analytical and mistrustful of their feelings than the working-class families, who almost without exception had accepted the child warmly and unconditionally as one of them. In the group discussions it came out that four or five middle-class mothers were surprised and guilty to find that the love they felt for their natural-born and for their adopted child was somehow different. They had accepted the adopted child as a member of the family, but did not feel that he was part of them in quite the same way that the others were. People had told them this would happen but they had not believed it. Husbands had been little help, as most did not share this feeling, and the wives were relieved to find that some other mothers also were experiencing this and felt guilty about it. They loved and enjoyed caring for the adopted child and said they had no regrets, but there was this 'difference' in their love. All agreed it was because they had not experienced the birth of the child, as they had with their other children, and had not cared for him as a helpless and dependent newborn baby. One wonders how much late placements contributed to this, and whether a totally dependent infant of a few weeks might have aroused the same sort of parental responsiveness they had felt for the children who were born to them. No one related the problem to difference in race, but only to adoption, so on a conscious level, at least, colour did not enter into the incomplete acceptance of the child. The only other study in which this phenomenon has been noted was done by Shaw and reported in the *British Journal of Psychiatric Social Work* in November 1953. Miss Shaw's study was not of interracial adoption, so the fact that her mothers with natural-born and adopted children 'admitted' a difference in the quality of their love toward these children could not possibly have been related to difference in race.

In one of our groups a woman who had natural-born children of her own, and also step-children, in addition to the adopted baby had been able to individualize them all and to recognize that she loved each in a somewhat different way. Discussion around this seemed to help some of the others to accept that one does not love any two persons in quite the same way, including one's natural-born children. It also helped to point out some of the ways in which adoption is different and what it is possible to expect of it and what is not possible.

Most adopters were pleased that their adopted child seemed similar in temperament to themselves or someone else in their family. Two couples who had found their child to be of a very different temperament which they did not understand, felt this had made the child less easy to love. Again, if difference in colour entered into this at all, there was no awareness of it. These two families did feel they had been given a child whose age and temperament were not entirely right for them, but that with the necessary expenditure of effort they had overcome earlier serious difficulties. Some other parents pointed out that even among natural-born children in a family, one child may be harder than the others to care for, and still others believed that difference in temperament between a child and his parents was not necessarily undesirable. Several people said their adopted child had been easier to care for than their other children.

A mother with one natural-born and one adopted child said she was sure from her experience with both children that there is no such thing as 'instant motherhood, whether natural or adopted', and she credited her adoption worker with being a kind of 'spiritual midwife', who had built an emotional bridge between the adopters and the baby. However, the couples without natural-born children said they immediately felt the adopted child was their very own and had contined to feel so. As they related some of the joys of parenthood, a father of four told them it is quite usual for parents to have moments of wishing they had never had the children, but that adoptive parents deny this because they think it would be wrong to feel like that even for a moment when they have wanted a child so much.

The meetings brought out a tendency by some English adopters to deny their child's colour, and to stress how much he looked like one of them, or to say he was growing lighter, or that people thought he was suntanned and did not recognize him as coloured. Sometimes the reality was fully accepted only after the very light child had grown noticeably darker during the second year or after being exposed to bright sunlight on holiday. Another English mother said it might be snobbish, but she was proud of her child's pure Indian background.

Some of the discussion about procedures in adoption was not especially productive. We wonder if there might have been more criticism of procedures if members of the staff had not been the group leaders. The adopters' reaction to the quality and duplication of services during the supervision period and their experience in the courts have been mentioned in Chapter 7. Most people had found the pre-application meeting helpful, as they had known almost nothing about adoption or what it might involve for them. Someone thought the meetings had made it all seem too easy, but others thought they had been prepared for the worst.

The family study had seemed unnecessarily long and thorough to some, and a few others were surprised at being offered a child so soon. It seemed to be agreed that the thoroughness of a family study creates

K

confidence in the total work of an agency, e.g. in work with the natural parents and the baby. Nearly everyone was glad to have had a chance to meet the baby without being expected to take him with them on the same day; they felt they needed a 'breathing space' between meeting and becoming parents to a child. They were very glad not to have been offered a choice of children, and the one family that had been told of three children found they worried later about the two they couldn't take. Someone said they had trusted the worker's choice just as she trusted them. An adoptive father was troubled by his visits to a residential nursery to get to know the child before taking her. He said, 'The nursery is upsetting; they all clamour for you; they all need somebody and you want to take them all.' Some adoptive mothers liked visiting the baby in a foster home and learning at first hand exactly how he was accustomed to being cared for. But one mother thought she would have found it hard to be told by a competent foster mother when she felt so ignorant of babies; she preferred to find out for herself. Some others for whom this was a first baby had scarcely been aware of the foster mother at all. Those who had not met her had given no thought to her, one adoptive father saying he would have felt her to be an intruder at that time, but now he was grateful to her for taking good care of the baby. They had been entirely wrapped up in their own feelings when getting to know the baby.

Most of the formerly childless couples would have been dismayed if they had been required to meet the child's natural mother at that time, but there were two who now rather wished they had, one because they were so sure they would have liked her and the other in order to be able to tell the child later that they had actually seen his first mother. Most couples with natural-born children reacted negatively to the idea that they might have met the mother of their adopted child, but here, again, there were a very few who in retrospect thought this might have been a good thing. The arranged meeting between one couple and the natural mother after legal adoption has been described in Chapter 6. Others in the same discussion group with this couple were anxious to hear about it, but no one wished for a similar opportunity. One mother said it could be disappointing and this could come through when talking to the child later about his first parents.

The adopters were almost unanimously in favour of early placement. They were agreed that they had committed themselves fully at the very beginning, that it was best for the child to be placed young, and they would carry on if later something were found to be wrong with the child. The couple mentioned in Chapter 7, who had been worried about their child's development, and the possibility of some physical or mental handicap, had not felt free to mention this until after the legal adoption, because they had heard of a judge withholding an Adoption Order because a child's health or development had been less than perfect. These adopters along with others stressed that they had taken the child for better or worse and felt he was completely theirs. As another adoptive mother said, 'Blood is not thicker than water after six months'. This applied also to the deep concern most of the adoptive parents had felt before the court hearing, that the mother might change her mind and reclaim the child. In the two cases where this had happened, adopters had taken another child some four months later, but they still spoke of the first child in the hushed tones one uses in speaking of the dead. In fact one of these adoptive parents had been obliged to return the child to the mother at the court hearing, and she said, 'It was just like a death really. Friends discouraged us from taking another child, but we felt our luck couldn't be that bad.' The older child in this family only accepted the second baby after the court hearing, because she was afraid the same thing might happen again. The other adoptive parents whose child was reclaimed after only a few days said it had been a shattering experience for their eldest daughter, a child of five, who had been well prepared for the new sister, then lost her, and could not believe the new one would stay. Details of these two situations have been given in Chapters 3 and 7.

Looking ahead, the adopters were most concerned about what the future might hold for their adopted child. Newspaper and television stories about racial discrimination and the adolescent problems of non-white children growing up in Britain had been rather alarming to some of the English adopters. However, there was considerable feeling in the groups that these adopted children would not experience the same problems as children in many immigrant families, because the adopted children had been born here, would be growing up as English children and would never have known any other way of life. The Asian, African and West Indian adopters tended to be optimistic about the future for children born and brought up in the British culture and differing from other Britons only in physical appearance. The English adopters believed adolescence would be the most difficult time, but they differed on what should be done about it. Everyone was sure the children would continue to be accepted by the extended family and their circle of friends to the extent that he was accepted by them now.

A few felt they should prepare the child to expect some prejudice and discrimination in the larger community so it would not come as a shock to him, but others thought it foolish to go out to meet trouble that might never happen. The latter intended to do everything possible to give the child a secure and loving home to steady him against whatever troubles life might bring including any discrimination, but they felt there was little more that could be done in advance. One English woman said they were all coloured families now and subject to possible discrimination, and that this should help them to understand how the child would feel if he should meet it. The non-European adopters felt the only way to keep oneself from being harmed by discrimination was not to go looking for it, and to ignore it if it should occur.

Conclusions from these Meetings
The discussions brought out some of the satisfactions of life with an adopted baby, which were much the same as the satisfactions accompanying the arrival of any wished-for child. The fact that in forty of the fifty-one families the child was of different race had not detracted from their pleasure in the child. Other youngsters in the family had welcomed the adopted baby and accepted him on an equal footing and in most cases with only a minimum of jealousy. Most grandparents had caused no trouble and indeed were being very supportive.

We learned about some minor incidents occasioned by the child's colour or his adopted status, but parents had coped with these very well, and in some families they had not been seen as problems at all but only as part of the ups and downs of life with a family of children.

Some mothers with natural-born children had found life with an adopted, non-white baby a little more difficult than they had expected, but they felt satisfied with the way they had been able to accept this challenge. They were inclined to relate any difficulties to the temperament of the child or his age at placement, but a few were concerned about their own inability (so far) to feel exactly the same toward this child as toward their natural-born children. The question remains as to whether a child, who is offered love and security in a family, will develop happily if the love he receives is not less, but somehow just a bit different from what other children in the family receive. Is this difference likely to grow greater or less as the years go on? Will it be able to withstand the strain of an adolescent's normal rebellion – or will the difference, by that time, have disappeared? Is the fact that the child looks different from the other children in the family a constant reminder that he was not always one of them? The adopters frequently said they tend to forget all about the difference in colour until the contrast with their other children suddenly brings it home.

The couples who had been childless were interested in the same things as most adoptive parents everywhere. They needed to feel the child was completely their own and were reluctant to have to share him with his former parents, even in fantasy. These feelings were the same regardless of the race of the adopters or the child. These new parents were finding their adopted child quite perfect and they reported the remarkable change the child had made in their lives. They saw the child as being like them in one way or another, and where they were of different race they tended to see the similarities rather than the differences. They were much more concerned at this time about how to introduce their child to the fact that he once had other parents, than they were about the problems adolescence might bring because of his race.

Many people expressed their enthusiasm for these discussions, as a means of exchanging experiences, sharing feelings, and testing out their ideas among others who had invested a good deal of themselves in this same venture. Nearly everyone participated actively and there was reluctance to end even after two hours of discussion. Some groups could easily have turned into fond parent chat or sessions on general child rearing. This sort of outlet may have been needed, as adopters often feel somewhat isolated from other parents, but the purpose of agency discussion groups is to focus on experiences and problems specific to adoption.

Each family had been seen at home shortly before the first meeting of their group. This occasionally made it possible for the leader to steer the discussion into a helpful area or into the sharing of a problem or unique experience. Conversely, a subject raised at a meeting and of particular interest to one member of the group could be pursued further with the caseworker at the next home visit. This led the staff to think that a combination of interviews and group discussions is a method that might be useful in adoption at almost any stage, e.g. during the family study and preparation for placement, or during the period between placement and legal adoption. Could some of the anxiety and tension of these periods be relieved by group discussion? Could interviews be focused more helpfully on material arising out of the groups?

In our group discussions the staff learned a little of how adoptive parents felt about the Project's methods and procedures, and adopters seemed to be helped by sharing their pleasures and problems, and possibly by modifying some attitudes and ideas that would help them to relax and enjoy their adopted child even more. There was interest in holding meetings when the children were older, and it did seem that groups held somewhat later might be even more beneficial. Agencies have held meetings for adoptive parents whose children were of various ages, though none as young as ours, we believe. An agency in New York[5] found ages three to seven best, and Alexina McWhinnie[6] in Edinburgh concluded that these discussions are most useful of all to people whose adopted children are well under five years old. In her groups Dr McWhinnie found that by the time a child was six his adoptive parents had taken up a particular stand on telling about adoption and what background information they would give him; they had already missed the chance to give adequate answers to the child's spontaneous questions, and were now sitting back waiting for the child to ask questions which he might never do. Since 'telling' is one of the most difficult problems for adopters, we too are inclined to believe that group discussions ought to be timed to be of most help to adopters in meeting this obstacle. Perhaps additional meetings when children are much older might be helpful, too, but if the 'telling' has been started wisely, fewer problems related to the adoption are likely to arise later.

REFERENCES

(1) Gochros, Harvey L., 'A Study of the Caseworker-Adoptive Parent Relationship in Postplacement Services', *Child Welfare*, Vol. 46, No. 6, June 1967, p. 325.

(2) Goodacre, Iris, *Adoption Policy and Practice*, Allen & Unwin, London, 1966.

(3) Gochros, *op. cit.*, pp. 317-25.

(4) Dr McWhinnie also found no one in her twelve Edinburgh groups who wished to remain anonymous. See McWhinnie, Alexina M., 'Group Counselling with 78 Adoptive Families', *Case Conference*, Vol. 14, No. 11, March 1968 and April 1968.

(5) Brown, Florence G., 'Services to Adoptive Parents after Legal Adoption', *Child Welfare*, July 1959.

(6) McWhinnie, *op. cit.*, March 1968, p. 410.

CHAPTER 9

FOLLOW-UP STUDY OF THE ADJUSTMENT OF THE CHILD IN THE ADOPTIVE FAMILY

Purpose and Plans

It was always planned to assess the placements at the end of the four-year Project, although the value of this would be limited by the age of the children and the short time since their adoption. As the desirability of obtaining information at a later date became increasingly obvious, the staff and committee began to plan that the follow-up interviews described here should be the first phase of a longitudinal study of the on-going adjustment of these children in their adoptive family and community. The present study was set up, therefore, with the probability that it would be part of a larger undertaking.

Very little was known about how interracial adoptions turn out, and the only work that might shed much light on this was a five-year study which was still in progress in the United States. This research involved ninety-seven American Indian children adopted by white families. The study was directed by Professor David Fanshel and was carried out in five semi-structured interviews held annually with the adoptive parents. It is hoped that this study, too, will be extended until the children have reached what is likely to be a more critical stage in their adjustment to family and community.

The purpose of the American Indian study was much the same as ours – to measure the outcome of the placements, particularly 'the degree to which these families and their children have become successfully integrated as nuclear families'.[1] Both studies hoped to answer such questions as: What has been the nature of the adopters' experience with these children? How are the youngsters faring in these homes? How has American (in our case British) society been able to accept interracial adoptions?

The children placed by the British Adoption Project were still so young that the present study could give only the most tentative answers to such questions. With one exception the children had not started school. Some were still babies, and most were too young to appreciate their racial difference or to have more than an elementary understanding of their adoptive status. Margaret Kornitzer, who did a very comprehensive follow-up study of children placed by five different agencies in Britain, says telling 'proves' the adoption.[2] Using this criterion, it can be said that it was too early for most of our adoptions to have been put to the test. Also, the position these children will be able to hold in their community will not be evident until they go to school, or perhaps even until adolescence. If our follow-up study is extended to include these later years, a good deal can be learned about what it is like for a coloured youngster in Britain to grow up as an adopted child, and whether this is very much harder for parents and child when they are of different racial origins. Two or three interviews about five years apart also would show whether a child had changed a great deal over time or was much the same kind of child as when he was younger.

Research Method

We were most fortunate in securing permission to adapt Professor Fanshel's tested questionnaire to our use. For the end-of-Project interviews our questionnaire was basically the same as his, except that several questions were omitted and some new ones added.[3] For example, information about the children's school adjustment was not relevant. The revised questionnaire contained eighty-six questions covering the adopted child's health and developmental progress, physical appearance, personality and general disposition, social and family relationships, family climate, problems attributable to the child's racial background or adoptive status, the parents' child rearing patterns and the family's plans for the future. Answers to questions were recorded by a tick or at most a few words of explanation. The questionnaire was intended to serve as the framework for a widely ranging discussion, but in practice, it was so long that very often almost the whole interview was taken up in completing the questionnaire. As a result, in instances where some of the answers were rather superficial, interviewers were unable to press further for important information or feelings which they already knew existed.

The adopters, themselves, were interested in the study, though some felt it had come so early that there was not much they could add to what the Project team already knew. One couple, particularly interested in social research, was critical of the lack of a control group which, of course, was a limitation of the study, although we did hope to make some useful comparisons between the interracial and intra-racial adoptions in the Project.

The entire group of fifty-one adoptive families was studied, and the number of adopted children involved also was fifty-one. Two children who had recently been placed as the second adopted child in a family were not included, because their situation was felt to be different. The interviews were all carried out between November 1968 and January 1969, and two families who were living overseas posted their questionnaire during that period. Most of the visits were in the evening in order to see the parents together and were made by appointment. This worked out well because the child was seen briefly before his bedtime, and the parents were free afterwards to give their full attention to the interview.

It was decided that advantages might outweigh the disadvantages if the interview with each family was carried out by the Project worker who knew that family best. The interviewers were to rate the results in terms of six main variables, using a scale employed by Fanshel in the American Indian study. To facilitate the rating, the material was summarized under six headings which had been defined by Fanshel as follows:

A. *Physical growth and development*

This covers the child's physical well being and developmental progress. In the realm of health, focus is upon the presence or absence of disabling health conditions. These include illnesses which may occur episodically as well as conditions of a long standing and chronic nature. The developmental conditions concern such phenomena as physical growth, walking, speech, sleeping, eating and elimination – all related to a perspective of the child as an emerging biological organism.

B. *Intellectual and cognitive competence*

This covers the child's intelligence and intellectual potential as revealed by the parents' reports of their impressions of his intelligence, his degree of alertness, his reading readiness, his performance in school (if he is in school). Include as a problem any condition which may jeopardize the child's present or subsequent school adjustment (e.g. low intelligence, thinking disorder, etc.).

C. *Personality characteristics and behavioural patterns*
This covers pathological elements in the child's personality including psychotic, pre-psychotic and neurotic states, as well as disturbances of character (character disorders). The presence of phobias, deep anxiety states, anti-social behaviour, extreme aggressiveness, and like behaviour should be noted as problems.

D. *Social relationships*
This covers the child's ability to develop satisfying social ties with other children as well as adults. The presence of self-isolating tendencies, the selection of inappropriate playmates, insecurity in social situations, excessive conformity, etc., should be regarded as problems.

E.1. *Family relationships*
This covers the ability of the adopted child to become integrated within the adoptive family. It refers to tendencies within him rather than the family attitude towards him (although these are difficult to separate). An adopted child may have problems if he feels the home is not permanently his, if he feels he has a second class status, or if he is painfully aware of the contrast in race between himself and his parents. Problems in relating to either parent or siblings or in accepting parental authority should be noted.

E.2. *Family climate*
This covers the ability of the adoptive family to integrate the child. It refers to tendencies in the total family towards him, rather than within him (although these are hard to separate). The family may have problems if they feel the child is not fundamentally theirs, if pressures on them, for example, tend to make them feel he is second class or if they are painfully aware that he is racially different from them. Problems in any members of the family in their relationship to the child, e.g. those concerned with authority, should be noted.

Report on Follow-up Interviews with Adopters
Thus far, the children had fared very well. All had had good physical care and the advantages of belonging to a family. Their health and development had been generally very satisfactory, and in most cases illness had been limited to occasional colds.

Seven parents commented on the small size (and sometimes the small appetite) of their Asian children, some registering slight irritation at this difference when it had caused a clinic or health visitor to query the child's diet. The parents of six other children felt they were growing faster than expected and were big for their age. One child was said to be overweight because she was 'a greedy eater'. One wonders if this child's eating habits may prove resistant to change. She was an overweight toddler when placed for adoption after spending nearly all her prior life in a residential nursery. We wondered if she might have developed a greedy attitude towards food as compensation for other satisfactions that babies have to be denied in a group living situation.

Ten of the children had had a 'skin rash', 'skin allergy' or 'eczema', all of them in English families, some of whom may not have known that the child's naturally dry skin requires frequent applications of oil. Eight adopters considered their child to have an unusual amount of energy, but four other families believed their child tired easily. The latter seemed more unusual to us than the child with boundless energy. One baby vomited frequently during his first weeks with new parents, but this had entirely cleared up and the child was thriving. As known at placement, one youngster required physiotherapy for a mild scoliosis, which had improved enough for discharge from the clinic after three months of treatment. Another child had a convulsion with high temperature at the age of two years, but quickly recovered and nearly three years later there had been no recurrence.

The only really serious problem of health or development was the difficulty another little boy had experienced in the use of his legs, which earlier seemed to be associated with a rather slow general development. Physical and developmental tests resulted in no definite diagnosis, but it was thought to be a mild hypotonia, which improved with physiotherapy. However, at the age of two years this youngster still did not have fully normal use of one leg and was frequently frustrated at not being able to keep up with the other active children in the family. His adopters quite naturally had found the lack of diagnosis hard to bear, but later they were relieved by his improvement and the knowledge that he would not have a serious handicap.

Some adopters believed the child had grown darker since he was with them, though in several cases this was so only in the summer when a child had darkened very quickly in the sun. Others saw the child as growing lighter. Only six of the children were thought to have even slight awareness of their colour. The oldest child in the Project, who was then five years old, went through a short period about six months earlier of wishing he were white. This same child was said to have recognized some very black people as 'different' before he was three years old, and recently was thought to recognize his similarity to Asian friends who visited his home. Another child, just three years old and the youngest in a family of five, liked being 'brown' probably because the two eldest siblings had felt it made him rather special. One little girl recognized her similarity to the second adopted child. Another little girl was aware that she was brown, but not that this made her different in appearance from her family. Another knew she had 'a better brown than mummy's suntan'. The sixth child, when told of her adoption and difference in colour at about two and a half, insisted she was not brown, so it was not mentioned again and her parents felt she had forgotten about it. Obviously, the full impact of colour had not been experienced yet by any of the Project children, but perhaps future interviews will show what connection there was between the manner of these early introductions to their colour and a healthy acceptance of it later on.

There were nine families where some member of the extended family (usually a grandparent) was not as completely accepting of the adoption as might be desirable, but this amounted only to a neutral or lukewarm attitude, rather than open hostility, except in the case where a complete break with the wife's parents had occurred earlier because of a mixed marriage. The general pattern had been for relatives to move from a wait-and-see attitude before placement to genuine acceptance or even enthusiasm when the child became known to them as a person. Again, it will be interesting to see how relatives outside the immediate family move in their feeling for these children as they grow older.

Three adoptive mothers were employed full time outside the home at the time of the follow-up. Their children were doing particularly well and were rated by both interviewers, as well as by the author and the outside rater, as making an excellent adjustment, while their adopters were rated as being particularly successful in integrating them into the family. In one of these families a grandmother lived in the home and cared for the child while the mother worked; in the second case a next-door neighbour, who was devoted to the child, cared for her; in the third instance it was a carefully chosen au pair girl, who took care of this youngster and another child in the family while the mother continued in her profession. These three families were all in different socio-economic groups and two of them were from the Caribbean. In three other English families the mother worked part time at home in a professional or semi-professional capacity, and in a fourth English family the mother had returned to part time teaching for a while, but had discontinued this work after the recent birth of another baby.

In five families a new baby had been born and in two more a birth was expected shortly. Three other families had adopted another child. (Two of these adopted children were placed by the Project and were of mixed race; in the case of the third family, no children of mixed race were available for adoption in the country to which they had emigrated.) Eighteen more families had decided to adopt a second coloured child; another nine were undecided about a second adoption, usually because the husband felt they could not afford it. Two families had taken a foster child and two others were daily minding a youngster. Thus, fourteen families had added another child to their household and eighteen more were planning to do so. These are, indeed, people who enjoy a home full of little children.

Various patterns of child rearing were shown in the follow-up study. A large number of fathers shared the care of the adopted child and many fathers played with the child regularly for their own pleasure. Various attitudes were shown towards discipline, and some felt the word did not even apply to such young children. However, 'no' was a frequently used word in most households, and many parents reported that they resorted to an occasional 'smack' to keep the child away from such dangers as electric sockets and appliances or a busy road. More than a third of the families reported that their adopted child was unusually sensitive to criticism. Could this be related to some lingering feeling of uncertainty about their place in these families, or were the parents perhaps particularly attuned to their adopted child's reactions? Only one or two said their handling of the child in public places was influenced by his racial difference; they felt that because they were conspicuous they were subject to quick criticism. The parents did not go out much for pleasure unless the children could go with them. Fourteen of them virtually never did so, and a few others went out only when there was a willing and available granny. Twenty said they left the child with a baby-sitter occasionally, but only seven did this as often as once or twice a week.

Relatively few problems of behaviour were found at this early stage of the children's development. The most serious, in our view, were those which were related to the interaction between parents and child, where adopters had found the child's temperament, developing personality or general disposition so different from their own that they were unable to understand or perhaps even to accept and love the child as deeply as they had hoped. Without exception we found parents working hard to make the adoption a success, although some seemed more able than others to enjoy the child.

The few unpleasant incidents encountered by the adopters because of a child's colour were disclosed more fully in the discussion groups than in these follow-up interviews. However, although forty of these adoptions were across racial lines, these adopters and children had been well accepted in their community during this period when the children were of pre-school age. The little boy who had started school was the only non-white child in his class. He was said to be getting along well with everyone, but the experience of such a passive little boy might not be predictive for other more aggressive and competitive youngsters.

Most of the parents felt they would like to keep in touch with the other Project adopters in one way or another, and two had already offered to take some responsibility for this – whether through meetings, correspondence or newsletters. However, only about a third were interested in future discussion groups, as there would be no member of the staff to lead them. There were two or three people who were opposed to any continuing contact as tending to make the adoption special or different.

Rating the Progress of the Adoptions

The ratings were done separately for the child and family with each child's overall adjustment rated on a scale from one to seven, and each family rated from A to E. Obviously, it was difficult to keep the assessment of child and parents as separate as one might wish. These were subjective judgements (with all the limitations of such judgements) about (1) the overall adjustment of the children up to the time of this study and (2) the quality of care the adopters had given the children, their strengths and weaknesses as parents, and their success in making the child a full member of the family. Fanshel explained the rating scale as follows:

Rating of child's overall adjustment

    1. Child is making an excellent adjustment in all spheres of his life – the outlook for his future adjustment is *excellent*.

2. Intermediate position.

3. Child is making an adequate adjustment – his strengths outweigh the weaknesses he shows – the outlook for his future adjustment is *hopeful*.

4. Intermediate position.

5. Child is making a mixed adjustment – generally the problems he faces are serious and the outlook for his future adjustment is somewhat *guarded*.

6. Intermediate position.

7. Child is making an extremely poor adjustment – the outlook for his future adjustment is *unpromising*.

Rating of adoption homes

Considering the problems the parents have had to face in caring for this child, make a judgement about the quality of the home. Try to keep your judgement independent from your assessment of the child.

A. Considering all information secured in the home interview, this seems to be the kind of home situation one would want a child to have – the kind in which a child would have the best opportunity for healthy development.

B. Intermediate position.

C. This relates to the kind of home situation in which some factors are not as one would like them to be, but they are not the kind that seem likely to be seriously harmful to the child.

D. Intermediate position.

E. Considering all information secured in the home interview, this seems to be the kind of home situation from which one would like to protect a child – the kind likely to interfere with his happiness and healthy development.

When the two interviewers worked with this rating scale, they did not use entirely the same frame of reference, so their ratings were not strictly comparable. One worker had taken into account everything known about the adoptions, while the other had tried with only limited success to keep to the findings of the interview and to discount what was already known about the families and children. Another difference in approach affected the scores, too. One worker tended to look for signs of possible future difficulties, while the other concentrated on the kind of adjustment the child and the family had been able to make up to that time, in spite of any problems they had brought with them to the adoption situation. Also, one worker applied the highest rating (1 and A) only to situations that seemed very nearly perfect, i.e. exceptional, while the other used this category more generously.

It probably was expecting the impossible for a worker to assess cases without using her prior knowledge of them, and so she could not rate her own and another worker's cases from the same starting point. Fanshel alone rated all the placements in the American Indian study, but had not placed the children or done any of the follow-up interviews. He made these judgements on the basis of his very considerable experience as a social worker in child welfare, then later asked some other adoption workers to rate a sample of his cases to test the reliability of his judgements.

In our own Project it seemed that some outside person with a wide knowledge of adoption, but no knowledge of these children or families, should rate them *on the basis of the follow up interviews alone*, and Miss Jane Rowe, Director of the Association of British Adoption Agencies, very kindly consented to do this. It also was decided that the author, who has had long experience of adoption work, should attempt to rate each adoption on the same scale, but *taking into account everything known about the children and adopters at the end of the Project*.

When both these ratings were done and compared, there was very close agreement between them on the children, but a little more variation on the families. Table 9.1 shows the independent rater's assessments in the vertical columns and the author's assessments in the horizontal columns. The forty children given exactly the same rating by the author and the independent rater are shown in the central diagonal cells in that Table. It can also be seen that there was only one point of difference in the assessment given to any of the children by the two raters, and that one rater did not give consistently higher ratings than the other. In the same manner, Table 9.2 compares the ratings given the adopters. Here thirty-five families were given the same rating by both. Again, one rater did not assess consistently higher or lower than the other, and there were only two instances where the difference was greater than one point. These latter two families were given A by the independent rater and C by the author, who had based her assessment on information not available in the follow-up interviews alone.

TABLE 9.1

Comparison of Ratings on Children

Author's ratings	Independent ratings						Total author's ratings
	1	2	3	4	5	6 and 7	
1	25	4					29
2	4	10					14
3			5	1			6
4					1		1
5				1			1
6 and 7							—
Total independent ratings	29	14	5	2	1	—	51

TABLE 9.2

Comparison of Ratings on Adopters

Author's ratings	Independent ratings					Total author's ratings
	A	B	C	D	E	
A	16	2				18
B	7	13	1			21
C	2	4	4			10
D				2		2
E						—
Total independent ratings	25	19	5	2	—	51

L

Each rater placed forty-three children (though not all the same ones) in category 1 or 2. Thus 84 per cent of the children were placed in categories which signified a very good adjustment. However, the outside rater considered forty-four of the fifty-one families (86 per cent) to be getting on very well as adoptive parents (categories A and B), while the author placed only thirty-nine of the families (76 per cent) in these categories. The children were still too young for any meaningful comparison of these figures with various follow-up studies that have been made of white children in adoptive homes.

The independent rater explained that she did not give a rating of 1 or A in any case where the follow up study showed that (1) the parents were not enthusiastic about the adopted child, (2) family relationships were not described as very happy, (3) close relatives living nearby were not fully accepting of the adoption, (4) parents were still doubtful or concerned about 'telling', (5) the parents described the child in critical or unsuitable terms. This rater also commented that she found it a handicap not to know a little more about the adopters and their other children, especially such information as the age and sex of the other children in the family. This information was not recorded on the interview schedules, but it was, of course, known to the author.

In considering everything the Project knew about the adoptions the author did her best to separate the adjustment of the child from the assessment of the home situation. Presumably, one could find well-adjusted children in not-so-good homes, or maladjusted children in good home situations, especially the latter since some adopters had been willing to cope with a child who had suffered early deprivation. Helen Witmer, in her follow-up study of independent adoptions in Florida, found that the homes rated as good were more likely to have well-adjusted children, but the correlation was not as high as might have been expected.[4] In our study only one child was rated more than one point higher than the family, and none more than one point lower. In the author's total Project ratings thare were only two children more than one point higher than their family and none more than one point lower. The best adjusted children were found in the 'best' family situations. When the interaction between the child and his parents had been positive, both the child and his adopters showed up high on the rating scale, but when the interaction had been somewhat negative the family as well as the child fell into a lower category.

The author used the same criteria as the outside rater, but having more information she was able to give added consideration to the quality of the mothering during these early years, and to see a child's behaviour as symptomatic of the quality of the parent-child relationship. Consideration was also given to whether a child and adopters were doing as well as could be expected, keeping in mind that some children were more difficult than others because of such things as age at placement or unfortunate pre-placement experiences. Particular attention was paid to the place the adopted child had made for himself in the family and to how well the parents had been able to accept and love him as their own and equally with any other children in the family. When difficulty was encountered in this area, it did not seem to be related to difference in colour but to a clash in personality or temperament. As only two of the non-white families already had other children, there were too few to allow us to judge from their experience whether a child of the same race as his adopters was more likely to be fully accepted in a family of natural-born children.

No child was placed in category 6 or 7 by either rater, as none of the children was making such a poor adjustment that the outlook for the future was very unpromising. However, there were three who seemed to both raters to be making a mixed adjustment with some fairly serious problems. These three children, placed in category 4 or 5 by both raters, were full Asian children aged four months to one year when placed in these families. Two were dark, one was light in colour, and all were generally thought to be nice-looking children. The adoptive parents of these children were English and already had a natural-born child close in age to the adopted child. All were rather idealistic and their wish to help a needy child figured prominently in their motivation to adopt. They had all had another child born to them since the adoption, and one wonders about the mixed feelings a woman might have in preparing for a natural-born child at the same time that she is struggling to develop maternal feelings toward the adopted child. The child, too, if still uncertain about his full acceptance, might be expected to react to having to share his parents with a younger, more dependent and obviously much loved baby.

No family was rated E at this time. Twelve, including the adopters of the three children just mentioned, received a rating of C or D by one or both raters. Ten of these were white families, two were non-white, and the proportion in social classes I through IV was similar to the proportion of each of these classes in the total group of adopters. However, among *the adopted children in these twelve families there were three times as many girls as boys and three times as many Asians as Africans and West Indians.* This is a larger proportion of girls and of Asians than in the overall group of adopted children.

The outside rater gave A-1 to twenty-one families and their adopted child, and the author gave this rating to fifteen, but there were only twelve who received it from both. *Analysing these twelve A-1 situations, we found that five families or two-fifths of these adopters were Asian, Negro or racially mixed couples,* whereas such families made up only one-fifth of all the Project adopters. Seven of the twelve were the only child in the family, but this is explained by the large proportion of non-white couples, most of whom were starting their family by adoption. *There were eight boys and only four girls in this group,* although boys constituted only two-fifths of the overall group of children in the study. *There also were twice as many Negro or part Negro children (eight), as there were Asian or Eurasian (four) among those rated A-1,* whereas in the total group of adopted children only just over one-third were of Negro background. Stated another way it can be said that *eight out of eighteen, or nearly one half of the Negro or part Negro children in the study were considered to be doing extremely well* and were in families who were also rated in the highest category. Breaking the A-1 group down *for social class, a larger proportion (one-third) was found in the Registrar General's Social Class III than might be expected,* as Social Class III constituted only just over a fifth of the overall group of adopters.

Summary of Ratings

According to both sets of ratings most of the children were doing very well (categories 1 and 2), and only three were at all a matter for concern at this time because of some aspects of their adjustment to life in their adoptive families. Nearly half the children of Negro or mixed Negro background, whether placed across racial lines or not, had made an especially good adjustment in their new family (category 1 by both raters), and none was among the very few children with problems. Are Negro children easier to raise at this early age? Do adopters who take Negro children have a greater tolerance than others? Our group is much too small to answer such questions, but they suggest further research.

A disproportionately large number of coloured parents had been successful in integrating their adopted child into the family, and so had adopters (whether white or coloured) in Social Class III, those in skilled manual occupations and routine clerical work. It is interesting that Fanshel also found that 'there was some tendency of individuals of lower socio-economic status to have children whose adjustment appeared to be somewhat better than those of higher social status'.[5] Only two family situations gave any real grounds for concern and even these had many positive aspects which might well take them into a higher category at the time of the next follow-up interviews.

Plans for Continuing Research
This first phase of the follow-up study brought us to the end of the Project with these children, but the children were still very young and their adjustment could change for better or worse as they go out into school and community. The problem of 'telling' had not arisen yet for most of these parents and some will find this a real test. Some parents may find an older child more difficult, but others may come into their own as parents a bit later. It is too early to know how well the schools, churches and community at large will accept these inter-racial families once the child becomes a real part of community groups. It is not known whether the strains and stresses of adolescence will be very much greater for non-white children in English families than for children growing up in an adoptive family of their own race. If, as is planned, this study is continued at intervals during the next fifteen to twenty years, answers to these questions can be sought with the willing co-operation of the Project adopters.

REFERENCES

(1) Fanshel, David, 'Indian Adoption Research Project', *Child Welfare*, November 1964, p. 486.
(2) Kornitzer, Margaret, *Adoption and Family Life*, Putnam, London, 1968, p. 226.
(3) See Introduction for availability of this questionnaire.
(4) Kelmer Pringle, M. L., *Adoption Facts and Fallacies*, Longmans, London, 1966, p. 62.
(5) Fanshel, David, *The Indian Adoption Research Project: Findings and Perspectives*, paper presented at the National Conference on Social Welfare, New York City, May 27, 1969. Privileged communication.

CHAPTER 10

AGENCY ADOPTIONS OF NON-WHITE
CHILDREN IN THE UNITED KINGDOM
– A QUANTITATIVE STUDY*

How many children of non-white or mixed racial heritage are there in Britain needing adoptive families? No one knew the answer to this question and estimates varied enormously. The Project decided to investigate the size of this problem because of its importance in any future planning for adoption services.

It was decided to try to learn how many adoptions of non-white children the British agencies had arranged in the course of a year, as well as how many additional children were not adopted because the agencies did not have families for them. The children reported here include those whose mothers and fathers, most of them unmarried, felt they could not provide a normal family life for their child and sought this through adoption, and some few others whose parents had virtually abandoned them to the long-term care of their local authority or children's society.

Research Method
Through the splendid co-operation of the children's officers, the voluntary adoption societies and diocesan moral welfare societies some interesting figures emerged from a postal questionnaire. Considerable effort was made in preparing the questionnaire[1] to avoid the same child being counted twice because of being known to more than one agency. With the help of the Secretary of the Church of England Committee for Diocesan Moral and Social Welfare Councils, it was possible to include the children the diocesan workers had been con-

* Reprinted with minor alterations from *RACE*, Vol. X, No. 2, October 1968, published for the Institute of Race Relations, London, by the Oxford University Press. Copyright 1968 Institute of Race Relations.

cerned about in their work with unmarried parents, but whom they were unable to offer to their own diocesan adoption societies or others because so few homes were available to these babies.

The response to the questionnaire was excellent. Returns were received from every one of the seventy-five registered voluntary adoption societies in the United Kingdom, and from 97·9 per cent of the 235 local authorities in the April 1967 Directory compiled by the Association of Children's Officers. These figures are for 1966, which was the most recent reporting year.

Adoption Orders for Agency-Placed Children

According to the agencies there were 13,122 Adoption Orders made in 1966 in the United Kingdom in respect of children whose placements had been arranged by them; 12,677 of these were white children and 445 (3·4 per cent of the total) were non-white, that is, of non-European or mixed racial heritage. Table 1 shows that the voluntary agencies placed 8,848 white children and 282 non-white; local authorities (both counties and county boroughs) placed 3,829 white and 163 non-white children. Thus the reports show that 3·1 per cent of all voluntary society placements and 4·1 per cent of all local authority adoption placements were of non-white children. Viewed in another way, the voluntary societies placed 69·8 per cent of the white children and 63·4 per cent of the non-white, while local authorities placed 30·2 per cent of the white children and 36·6 per cent of the non-white.

TABLE 10.1

Adoption Orders in the United Kingdom, 1966: Statutory and Voluntary Agency Placements

	White	Non-white	Total
Local authorities	3,829	163	3,992
Voluntary societies	8,848	282	9,130
Total	12,677	445	13,122

Of the 445 non-white children who were legally adopted through agencies, 421 were in England and Wales and 24 in Scotland.

Using the ten Standard Census Regions for England and Wales it can be seen in Table 10.3 that in every one of these Regions voluntary or statutory agencies, or both, had been able to place some non-white

TABLE 10.2

Adoption Orders, 1966, Divisions of United Kingdom: Statutory and Voluntary Agency Placements

	White	Non-white	Total
England and Wales	11,153	421	11,574
Northern Ireland	239	0	239
Scotland	1,285	24	1,309
United Kingdom	12,677	445	13,122

children for adoption. As might be expected, London and the South Eastern Region placed by far the greatest number, reflecting the need in the London area and to some extent the concentration of voluntary agency headquarters there. Since some of the voluntary agencies serving all of England and Wales do not keep figures of the region in which white and non-white children are available or are placed for adoption, we could not allocate these by region and they appear as a separate group in Tables 10.3 and 10.5. It should be noted in Table 10.5 that the children of these national societies make up more than half (52·3 per cent) of all the non-white voluntary society adoptions.

TABLE 10.3

Adoption Orders, 1966, Standard Regions of England and Wales: Statutory and Voluntary Agency Placements

	White	Non-white	Total
Northern	598	7	605
East and West Ridings	962	24	986
North Western	1,506	47	1,553
North Midland	818	24	842
Midland	875	21	896
Eastern	422	13	435
London and South Eastern	1,496	112	1,608
Southern	596	16	612
South Western	776	12	788
Wales	381	7	388
	8,430	283	8,713
National voluntary societies	2,723	138	2,861
	11,153	421	11,574

TABLE 10.4

*Adoption Orders, 1966, Standard Regions of England and Wales:
Statutory Agency Placements only*

	White	Non-white	Total
Northern	74	2	76
East and West Ridings	177	9	186
North Western	272	14	286
North Midland	268	15	283
Midland	308	10	318
Eastern	255	13	268
London and South Eastern	826	71	897
Southern	333	13	346
South Western	351	4	355
Wales	181	6	187
Total England and Wales	3,045	157	3,202

TABLE 10.5

*Adoption Orders, 1966, Standard Regions of England and Wales:
Voluntary Adoption Societies only*

	White	Non-white	Total
Northern	524	5	529
East and West Ridings	785	15	800
North Western	1,234	33	1,267
North Midland	550	9	559
Midland	567	11	578
Eastern	167	0	167
London and South Eastern	670	41	711
Southern	263	3	266
South Western	425	8	433
Wales	200	1	201
	5,385	126	5,511
Ten national voluntary societies	2,723	138	2,861
Total England and Wales	8,108	264	8,372

Foster Home Adoptions

We asked the agencies how many of the reported children had been adopted by families with whom they had first been placed for fostering, as it was known that some children achieve adoption in this way. It was found (see Table 10.7) that 45·6 per cent of the non-white children were adopted by people who had first boarded them as foster children compared with only 13·2 per cent of the white children. This is a very significant difference. Does it reflect only the scarcity of adoptive homes for non-white children or the agencies' uncertainty about them in an adoption situation?

TABLE 10.6

Children Adopted by Foster Parents, 1966

	White	Non-white	Total
England and Wales	1,441	197	1,638
Northern Ireland	58	0	58
Scotland	180	6	186
Total: United Kingdom	1,679	203	1,882

TABLE 10.7

Percentage of Adoptions by Foster Parents

Agency	Total Adoptions		Foster parent adoptions		Percentage adopted by foster parents	
	White	Non-white	White	Non-white	White	Non-white
Children's Departments	3,829	163	1,432	119	37·4	73
Voluntary societies	8,848	282	247	84	2·8	29·8
Totals	12,677	445	1,679	203	13·2	45·6

Of the children adopted through local authorities 73 per cent of the non-whites were adopted by their foster parents compared with only 37·4 per cent of the whites. In the voluntary agencies only 29·8 per cent of the non-white children and 2·8 per cent of the white children were adopted by their foster parents (see Table 10.7). Most of the voluntary adoption societies with the exception of the three large national children's organizations and the Catholic Rescue Societies do not provide foster home care to children, so these two groups account for virtually all of the foster parent adoptions in the voluntary societies.

Adoption of children placed by local authorities as foster children seems to be widespread and doubtless is due in part to the fact that some local authorities have not registered as adoption agencies. It is not known how many registered agencies choose this method for children they find hard to place for adoption, with the hope that foster parents will become so committed to a child that they will want to make him a full member of their family. Perhaps some agencies more often think of long-term fostering, and adoption just happens when a combination of circumstances in the child's biological family and in his foster family makes adoption desirable. It may be that in some instances parents do not come to a decision for adoption until the child is well settled in a foster home. If the foster parents then want to adopt him and the home can be approved, the child has had the advantage of getting settled early in the family that is to be permanently his.

Since many children do achieve adoption after first being fostered by the people who later adopt them, this method of finding families for children should be studied and the 'success' of these adoptions compared with a group of similar children placed by agencies directly into adoption homes. This would not be easy because of the considerable difficulties in agreeing upon what constitutes 'success' in adoption and how to measure it reliably.

Foster parents are often older and less well off financially than other adopters and most of them already have children. If it should be shown that when they adopt a foster child they make very satisfactory adoptive parents, it might lead to some revision of the arbitrary requirements agencies often set up for their adoptive applicants. This might open up the possibility of adoption to some children who otherwise would spend their childhood without close family ties because adopters have not been found for them. On the other hand, if study showed these adoptions to be lacking in important factors such as full acceptance of the child and his individuality in contrast with direct placement adoptions, the procedure of choice would be clear.

Children Not Offered for Adoption

We asked the children's departments and the diocesan moral welfare workers to tell us if there were non-white children known to them during 1966 who were not even offered to their adoption department or to voluntary agencies because they knew no adopters could be found for them. Unfortunately, most agencies do not keep statistics concerning the people they are unable to serve, so we had to be content with an estimate. Many agencies explained that their estimate was minimal. Some suggested that the improbability of adoption for a non-white child was so well known in their community that parents of such a child would not seek adoption, but would make do with some less satisfactory plan. Of course, these do not show in our figures.

However, the agencies did know of at least 415 children in 1966 whom they might have expected to place for adoption but for their racial heritage. This is nearly as many as the 445 who did achieve adoption during the year. Of these 415 children, 149 had come to the attention of diocesan moral welfare workers in England and Wales and 266 to local authorities. Table 10.8 shows the distribution of such children in the United Kingdom and the ratio of these to the number of Adoption Orders in each region.

Although in all areas of the United Kingdom there were children

TABLE 10.8

Adoption Orders and Children Not Offered for Adoption: Non-White Children, 1966

	Adoption orders†	Not offered‡	Ratio of children* not offered to adoption orders
Northern	7	12	1: 1·71
East and West Ridings	24	46	1: 1·92
North Western	47	23	1: 0·49
North Midland	24	17	1: 0·71
Midland	21	65	1: 3·10
Eastern	13	10	1: 0·77
London and South Eastern	112	183	1: 1·63
Southern	16	22	1: 1·38
South Western	12	13	1: 1·08
Wales	7	11	1: 1·57
Northern Ireland	0	3	—
Scotland	24	10	1: 0·42
Total	307†	415‡	1: 1·35*

* Two factors seriously detract from the accuracy and meaning of these ratios:

† The total number of Adoption Orders for non-white children as reported by the agencies was 445, but 138 of those placed by the national societies could not be allocated to regions and therefore are not included here.

‡ The figures in the 'Not offered' column are estimates and frequently said to be minimal.

the agencies had not been able to place for adoption, the problem was most pressing in absolute numbers in London and the South Eastern Region (particularly London) with nearly three times the Midland Region, which was second highest, and nearly four times the East and West Ridings of Yorkshire. The lowest number in the United Kingdom was in Northern Ireland; the lowest in England and Wales was the Eastern Region. Relatively, however, the position looked rather more serious in the Midlands, where there were at least three non-white children not offered for adoption for every one who was adopted. The figures do not tell us which regions were more successful, as a small ratio in Table 10.8 could mean either that very few of these children needed adoption in 1966 in that region or that agencies were not aware of a larger need. The only conclusion that can be drawn is that the non-white children adopted in 1966 through the efforts of the agencies were approximately half the number the agencies would have placed if families had been readily available to adopt them.

TABLE 10.9

Non-White Children Needing Adoption on Last Day of the Year

	Children's Depart- ments	Voluntary Societies	Moral Welfare Workers	Total
Northern	2	18	0	20
East and West Ridings	26	8	11	45
North Western	13	22	19	54
North Midland	29	9	0	38
Midland	54	69	11	134
Eastern	13	4	1	18
London and South Eastern	192	87	44	323
Southern	11	9	6	26
South Western	4	11	1	16
Wales	6	8	1	15
National Adoption Societies	—	98	—	98
Total England and Wales	350	343	94	787
Northern Ireland	3	0	—	3
Scotland	44	12	—	56
Total United Kingdom	397	355	94	846

Children in Need of Adoptive Homes on the Last Day of the Year
The number of non-white children known to agencies in the United
Kingdom as needing homes on the last day of the reporting year (846)
was more than twice as high as the estimated number not offered for
adoption during the year (415). The end of the year figure is more
likely to be reliable because each of these children was actually on an
agency's files on a particular day. It includes the national voluntary
societies whose work we have not been able to break down into
regions.

Table 10.9 shows that 397 of the 846 children needing placement at
the year's end were known to children's departments, 355 to voluntary
societies and 94 to moral welfare workers. Many of the voluntary
adoption societies do not have a list of children awaiting homes, as
they accept only those for whom they have families. In fact, 282 of the
343 (79·4 per cent) known to voluntary societies in England and
Wales at the end of the year were in the care of the large national
children's societies and the Catholic Rescue Societies. The agencies
had not given up hope of adoption for these children. No doubt many
of them found adopters during 1967, but only a little over half this
number (52·6 per cent) was placed in 1966, so it is clear that if they
were all to find homes, the scale of the agencies' work would have to
be nearly doubled.

Additional Factors
We asked agencies if there were other factors in addition to racial
background that might make it particularly difficult to place some of
these children for adoption – factors which might preclude adoption
even if the child were not of a minority race in Britain. Table 10.10
shows the results of this study.

Although Table 10.10 shows a total of 602 complicating factors,
the number of individuals involved is 457 because some children
presented more than one deterrent to adoption. Thus 457, or 54 per
cent, of the total 846 children known to be needing adoption on the
last day of the year presented at least one factor in addition to colour
that made it difficult to find adopters for them. In Scotland nearly
86 per cent of the forty-eight children had at least one complicating
factor. Thus, the problem in many situations goes beyond the fact
of racial difference.

By far the most frequent problem was the age of the child. Two
hundred and forty-six children were past the age at which the agency

TABLE 10.10

Additional Factors Complicating Adoption of Non-White Children Needing Adoption on Last Day of the Year

	Medical problems		'Bad' family history		Slow development		Age past infancy		Legal complications		Other factors		Number of children involved	
	LA.	VS.	LA.	VS.	LA.	VS.	LA.	VS.	LA.	VS.	LA.	VS.	LA.	VS.
England and Wales	49	12	85	14	34	8	107	109	47	5	49	5	266	140
Northern Ireland	1	0	1	0	0	0	1	0	0	0	1	0	3	0
Scotland	12	1	13	0	13	0	24	5	3	0	3	0	42	6
	62+13		99+14		47+8		132+114		50+5		53+5		311+146	
	75		113		55		246		55		58		457	

LA. = Local Authorities   VS. = Voluntary Societies

finds it least difficult to find adopters. One hundred and thirteen children had a 'bad' family history. We did not define 'bad' but wanted it to include whatever history an agency found a deterrent to placement. One wonders if it is the agency workers or prospective adopters who decide the history is too 'bad', as sometimes adopters may be willing to take more known risks than agencies realize.

There were seventy-five children with physical or medical problems. We do not know the nature or severity of the problems. We do know that placement of children with medical problems is often possible, but it requires rather special qualities in adopters and may result in parental experiences that vary according to the seriousness of the child's defect.[2] It is likely to take longer to find homes for these children and one wonders how many may be the same children for whom age had added another handicap.

Fifty-five of the children were showing 'slow development', a known deterrent to adoption. We do not know whether congenital factors made it advisable to postpone adoption placement until a child's development could be observed, or whether in some instances poor development might be the child's response to an unstimulating environment where he had no feeling of belonging. When the latter is the case, one supposes such a child might have been adopted at an early age but his chance has now passed, as age and slow development are added to his handicaps. There were legal complications in the situations of fifty-five children and again one can only hope that expert legal opinion can be obtained before the child begins to react unfavourably to the uncertainty of his situation or grows too old to appeal to most adoptive applicants.

Conclusions

Like so many studies, this one raised as many questions as it has answered. However, it does give some idea of the size and distribution of the problem of adoption for non-white children in Britain, and some picture of the extent to which the agencies are meeting it. The number placed directly by the mother or adopted through third parties, or by relatives, is not included in this study which was concerned with the problem as seen by the agencies.

It is encouraging to find that although non-white children constituted only 3·4 per cent of agency adoptions, efforts were made in very many agencies all over Britain with the result that 445 children in one year did find adoptive families. Forty voluntary and seventy-one statutory agencies were involved in the placement of these 445 children and many others could not have been expected to place any for, as they say, they never see a coloured child in their area.

The problem does not seem so vast as to be impossible of solution, although it presents a fairly serious problem in a few areas. Perhaps knowing that many agencies find homes for some of these children will encourage others to try. Certainly, there is no indication from this study that it cannot be done and much to show that it can. If 445 can be placed in spite of acute shortage of staff in many agencies, it appears that with a little increase in staff more could be done to attract applications for these children and to maintain flexible eligibility requirements; at the same time parents could be helped to reach their decision for adoption early while the child is most placeable.

Many of these children will be adopted by white British families, who will need some of the same high qualities of heart and mind that we found among the Project adopters if they are to cope with whatever unknown problems may lie ahead. Often these qualities may be found among applicants who are ruled out by agency regulations made long ago to keep the number of adoptive applicants to a manageable size. In the light of changing needs and circumstances, some agencies may want to review their practice of accepting only childless couples or certified church attenders, home-owners or members of certain social classes,[3] in favour of evaluating their applicants more on their readiness to accept as their own a child whose appearance and heritage are completely different from their own.

REFERENCES

(1) See Introduction for availability of these forms.
(2) Massarik, Fred, and Franklin, David S., *Adoption of Children with Medical Conditions*, Children's Home Society of California, Los Angeles, Calif., 1967.
(3) Goodacre, Iris, *Adoption Policy and Practice*, Allen & Unwin, London, 1966, pp. 35-6.

M

CHAPTER 11

THE ADOPTION RESOURCE EXCHANGE

Background to the Adoption Resource Exchange (ARE)

The provision of a co-ordinating service had been built into the British Adoption Project by the founders and was provided from the beginning of the Project. For the first two years we attempted to keep a Register of children and applicants who lived outside our geographic area, or for one reason or another could not be included in the Project's own placement programme. We soon became aware of the unfortunate lack of trust between many agencies and, indeed, the lack of any meaningful communication between them. Applicants and children were often in different parts of the country and remained unknown to each other. Some agencies were desperately seeking adopters, while others were turning them away because they had no such child needing a home. It seemed to us that geography and the wide range of standards and procedures among the agencies were important factors in the inadequacy of adoption services for coloured children.

Through our informal Register we occasionally were able to put two agencies in touch, so that a child and an appropriate family were brought together, but it was only in a very limited number of situations that a satisfactory placement was achieved. Potential adopters were lost because some of the agencies to which we referred them, unfortunately, did not know how to handle them and the applicants became discouraged. Sometimes when an inquiring family was referred to an agency which had children needing placement, the agency acted as if this were an approved home, and offered a child without securing any information about the family except that the British Adoption Project had received a letter of inquiry from them. In the case of some of the babies on the Register, we found that the natural parents' wish for adoption had not been explored thoroughly and they reclaimed the child after adoption placement, or made other permanent plans for him at the same time that we were trying to find him a home through the Register.

Workers in some of the agencies had had so little experience in placement of non-European children, that they did not know what information would be important or how to give what information they did have, e.g. in relation to a child's colour. Later we learned that, unwittingly, we had suggested an interracial child, who looked white, to a family who had asked for 'a little black boy' and who wanted just that. Some other combinations we suggested to the agencies were inappropriate because of our limited knowledge of the child and the would-be adopters.

We became deeply concerned about what we were doing in trying to give this service, and at mid-point in the Project it was decided to find out from the agencies involved just what the outcome had been from each suggestion we had made regarding families and children listed on the Register. The reports received from the agencies did nothing to increase our confidence in the work with the Register. It was clear that the Project simply did not have sufficient staff to provide liaison to an unlimited number of voluntary adoption societies, local authorities and moral welfare workers, and that the liaison service itself did not have the necessary structure. Yet there was an obvious need for some effective way for agencies all over Britain to co-operate in finding homes for non-European children, and some way to ensure that potential adopters of these children would not be lost in the confusing maze of agencies with their various requirements. We began to consider whether an Adoption Resource Exchange might be the answer to this need.

The failure of the Register to achieve its purpose had pointed up once again the complexities in adoption work. We had tended to over simplify, when only the broad outlines of a case were known, but again it became clear how much more adoption involves than bringing together any child needing a home and some family that has asked for a child. Furthermore, this was found to be more complex, not less so, when two or more agencies were involved.

Organization of the ARE

The Adoption Committee of International Social Service of Great Britain rather reluctantly agreed that the Register should be discontinued, but was enthusiastic about the idea of an Adoption Resource Exchange for the United Kingdom, when this was suggested. The Committee saw this as a natural outgrowth of the British Adoption Project, and a member offered to secure funds to underwrite temporarily the employment of another qualified adoption worker on a half time basis to get the new service off the ground.

The new Exchange was planned as an enabling body through which adoption agencies could work together to ensure that (1) those non-white children for whom adoption was the plan of choice were not denied this because the agencies working in their area could not find adopters for them, and (2) adoptive applicants seeking a non-white child, or able to accept one, were not lost because they could not find their way to an agency with such a child ready for placement. It seemed essential that participation in an Adoption Resource Exchange should be *voluntary and on an agency membership basis*, so that the members would have a share in establishing and carrying out its policies and programme, that it would, in effect, be *their* organization. From experience with the Register we knew the importance of the new scheme starting in a small, unpretentious way. We thought that perhaps a few really interested agencies could agree upon standards and procedures and thus establish the kind of mutual confidence so necessary in working together.

In the spring of 1967 we talked individually with the heads of staff in six agencies (three voluntary and three statutory), who we knew were deeply concerned about the problem, and found them all interested in developing some way of co-operating to overcome the shortage of homes for non-European children. The voluntary agencies involved were the Agnostics' Adoption Society, Dr Barnardo's Homes and the Guild of Service (Edinburgh); the statutory agencies were Birmingham, Oxford City and Somerset Children's Departments. Next, a meeting was called of the people responsible for the actual adoption work in these agencies. This group met several times, and with leadership provided by the British Adoption Project, formulated basic standards which they agreed to use in all their work relating to the Exchange. With these standards they believed they could feel confident in working together on placements. This group then met several more times and worked out procedures which they agreed to use for registering children or approved applicants with the Exchange, for considering combinations of child and family suggested by the Exchange, and for introducing and placing a child with adopters. This done, forms were drawn up to facilitate these procedures and to make sure the Exchange would have the information necessary to suggest families for children.

It was decided that families would not be registered with the ARE until they had been studied and approved by a member agency and were considered ready to be offered a child. The agencies agreed they would not hold an approved home indefinitely in case they might need it at some future time, but would make it available to a child from somewhere else by registering the family with the Exchange. Children, too, must be well known to the agency registering them and must be ready for adoption, with a medical examination completed, and background history already secured. With this information about children and approved adopters in hand many of the problems that had beset the old Register could be avoided. The registering agency would explore the firmness of the natural parents' decision to have the child adopted and would continue to try to find suitable adopters after registering the child with the Exchange. It was emphasized that the ARE should not be a substitute for imaginative development of adoption resources by each agency, but should be something to fall back on, when in spite of their best efforts member agencies have been unable to find adopters for a particular child or when they have no suitable child to offer to a family they have approved as adopters.

These original six agencies decided that member agencies should pay a small annual fee, which as the Exchange grows, will make it partially self-supporting. These fees have been approved by the ISS Adoption Committee, which acts as Administrative Committee for the Exchange. The six founding members also were asked to serve as an *ad hoc* committee on standards and procedures during the period that these were being tested and revised. As additional agencies were invited to consider membership, the requirements, responsibilities and benefits of the Exchange were discussed with the adoption officer, and usually with the children's officer or agency director, as well, to make certain the agency was in sympathy with the aims of the Adoption Resource Exchange and could work to the standards established by the members.

Present Programme

It was not until the spring of 1968 that the Exchange was ready to begin recommending placements of children. By that time it had twenty members and a half-time organizing secretary. When the British Adoption Project came to an end a year later, the Exchange had accomplished the placement of eleven of the forty-five children registered by member agencies, and the pace was accelerating as members learned from experience how to work together. The first child was placed in May 1968 and was legally adopted.

Of these first eleven children placed through the Exchange, five were Asian boys, two were Asian girls, one an African Negro boy and three were West Indian Negro girls. All but three were of mixed racial parentage. Nine were under six months when they went to adopters; the other two were eighteen and nineteen months when registered with the Exchange and twenty-two months when they went to adoption homes. The placements were all interracial, and each child has gone to a family with other adopted or natural-born children.

Member agencies became increasingly aware of the importance of early placement and began to register babies with the Exchange at an early age. Several subsequently were able to find adopters for their babies and withdrew the registration, so they were not depending exclusively upon the Exchange to find homes, but were continuing their own recruitment of adopters, as it had been hoped they would do.

The Exchange acted as an inquiry centre since its inception and up to April 1969 had received over two hundred inquiries from would be adopters of non-white children. These provided applications for member agencies in many parts of the United Kingdom. Those which were approved, but not needed locally, were registered with the Exchange, like any other approved adopters seeking a child. We think the processing of inquiries by the Exchange may have eliminated a good deal of frustration and delay for applicants. We also hope it has reduced some of the duplication of effort by the agencies, and has lessened the amount of travel for workers in some member agencies, who previously had been going far afield for homes. Best of all, it has added to the number of approved applications.

The ARE prepared a simple, illustrated leaflet to be sent in response to inquiries, which explains in question and answer form how adoption agencies work through the Exchange to bring adopters and babies together, and what is involved in applying to a member agency. The organization is in a unique position to know what kinds of homes are needed at any particular time, and publicity will be planned and focused accordingly.

In the quarterly meetings of the membership, the staff of the British Adoption Project shared some of the knowledge and skills derived from the Project, especially in such areas of the work as discussion groups for adoptive parents and assessment of applications from people of different racial or cultural background. Considerable meeting time also was devoted to clarifying and improving procedures in the light of experience.

Plans for the Future

The Adoption Resource Exchange has already demonstrated that it can serve as a useful vehicle in bringing babies and adopters together, with certain safeguards to both. It has shown that by learning to work together agencies can provide better service for their clients than they could attain by working in isolation.

The time has come for expansion, so that a larger number of adoption agencies can more nearly meet the needs of their non-European children or can provide families for children living in another area. Plans formulated by the membership in March 1969, if carried out, will double the number of members to forty by the end of 1970. Difficulties may be greater with a much larger membership, as agency representatives will not be able to know each other so well, but this should not be a serious problem if the standards already agreed are adhered to. There is nothing in the set up of the Exchange that precludes the possibility of extending it to include any children the agencies find hard to place because of their special needs, e.g. children with serious medical problems or handicaps, older children, brothers and sisters. Indeed, we hope that an active and well established Adoption Resource Exchange will want to extend its services to all children with special needs in adoption, though just now as an extension of the work of the British Adoption Project it seems appropriate to provide the service specifically for non-European children.

Looking to the future, the Adoption Resource Exchange is expected to help in narrowing the gap between the non-European children (and perhaps other so-called hard-to-place children) needing adoption and the number agencies have been able to place, but we foresee some additional benefits as well. Improved understanding and co-operation between adoption agencies can be expected to replace the former isolation, and, indeed, already has done so for the twenty member agencies. More will be learned about placing children for adoption across racial lines, but much should be learned, too, about how to recruit and assess adopters from the non-white races in Britain.

As social workers learn to place children who are of minority race in this country, they will be better able to extend their skills to finding homes for other children who also are hard to place. Perhaps most important is the probability that the good standards required to work through the Exchange will come into general use in the adoption work of member agencies. If standards established for placement of children with special needs should become general in the placement of all children, the result – as the Exchange grows in size – would be a very considerable overall improvement in British adoption services.

CHAPTER 12

CONCLUSIONS AND IMPLICATIONS FOR PRACTICE

Children who are of minority race in Britain today *can* find adoptive parents who will love and cherish them. This is the Project's chief conclusion and all the others relate to ways of accomplishing it.

Size of the Problem

Our survey of the problem revealed that 445 non-white children, who had been placed by agencies in the United Kingdom, were legally adopted in 1966, but this was only about half the number the agencies said they would have placed if homes had been more readily available. Unfortunately, there was no record of still others who had been refused placement because of the difficulty of finding adopters. It would be well if agencies would record all requests for service including the person's race, so that unmet needs could be identified more accurately. Some people feel that recording the race of agency clients seems divisive, but surely this depends upon the reasons for recording it.

For the children in the survey, the placement problem was not entirely one of colour, as more than half the non-white children known to be awaiting homes had additional deterrents to adoption, such as age, medical or legal problems, 'bad' family history, or slow development. A great many of these were older children, and their placement was sometimes complicated by one or more of these other factors. The survey also showed the extensive use that agencies had made of fostering as a possible avenue to adoption for non-white children. Nearly half the coloured children were adopted by people who had first fostered them for a local authority or a children's society, while this was true of only a very much smaller proportion of the white adoptions. So little is known about the long-term results of foster parent adoptions and how the success rate compares with other adoptions, that some research into this method should be undertaken without delay.

There were only a few areas of the country where a very large number of non-white children was needing adoptive families, but the agencies' lack of experience was often a serious problem in placing even a few children. We hope the work of the British Adoption Project and our detailed account of it in preceding chapters will lay the basis for a useful body of knowledge about adoption of non-European children.

Children and Natural Parents

It is very important that these children should be individualized and not thought of all together under the general label of 'coloured'. This emphasizes their difference in appearance from other Britons, but tells nothing else about them that is helpful in working with their parents or in finding adopters. We learned that unmarried parenthood has very different connotations for people from different cultural backgrounds, and even the word 'adopted' does not mean the same thing all over the world. As might be expected, it was found that both cultural and psychological factors entered into the parents' decision to keep or relinquish their children for adoption. We became more and more convinced that only a real understanding of what a child means to his parents, at this particular time in their lives and against the background of their cultural heritage, can enable anyone to make an accurate assessment of the finality of the mother's decision and to assess whether adoption is likely to be the best plan.

Our numbers were small, but these mothers who were planning for their non-white babies to be adopted clearly tended to make this decision early and were anxious to make the consent final. In fact, all but 10 per cent of the Project mothers were ready to give their final consent by the time the baby was six weeks old. The advantages of early placement to both the child and his adopters are well known, but the emphasis in Britain has been on repeated confirmation of the mother's decision to have her child adopted. We feel that a mother should be allowed to sign her final and legal consent *whenever she is ready to do so* after the child's birth.

We think an adoption agency's willingness to place a child for adoption should not be contingent upon an adoption home being immediately available. In the case of a coloured child, there often is no suitable home approved and waiting, and considerable effort may have to be made to find one. Meanwhile, who is to take care of the baby? We feel it is expecting a great deal of most mothers to be forced to care for a child for several weeks or months when they expect to relinquish the child afterwards. We saw instances where the effect of this was to punish a young mother by creating an impossible situation for her both practically and emotionally. Voluntary adoption societies should make suitable provision for temporary care, but at present only a few do this. Some local authorities are able to provide temporary accommodation for a baby during the period when an adoption home is sought, but others do not consider that such a child is in need of care. Often it is left to a moral welfare worker, with her extremely limited resources, to find a temporary foster home for the baby.

We found, too, that sometimes agency representatives may need to examine their own attitudes to illegitimacy, adoption and race. Some workers who referred children to the Project only reluctantly accepted a mother's decision to have her child adopted – or to keep him after all – and seemed to have particularly strong personal feelings involved when a baby was coloured. Mothers sometimes had to insist that a home must be found, after first being told this was impossible. It would be well, too, if more effort were made to secure background information from fathers and to include them in the planning for their children. When a father is living abroad, he could be interviewed through ISS, who also could explore the possibility of the paternal family making a home for the child in cases where this might be desirable. We question the practice of seeking only financial support from natural fathers. It was our experience that immigrant fathers quite often took a responsible attitude toward their out-of-wedlock children and wanted to be involved in plans for their care.

The natural parents of the children placed by the Project wanted them to have a warm and loving family, but most did not mind about the adopters' race or religion. Few of them were practising Christians and they did not require this of the adopters. Some were Muslim, Hindu or Buddhist. Knowing this, perhaps some agency committees will review their policies and make sure that no child is deprived of a family because of religious requirements set up for adopters a long time ago and in quite different circumstances.

The Project found that Asian children, especially healthy young baby girls, were quite easily placed for adoption. Recently, many agencies have been quite successful in finding homes for these children. In our experience fewer people wanted to adopt an African or West

Indian child of Negro or mixed racial parentage, but quite possibly a more focused recruitment effort would have produced more applications for these children. Families who did take Negro or part Negro children through the Project have found them very rewarding, and so far the children have made an excellent adjustment. Many Negro and racially mixed children are growing up in foster homes and institutions because it has been assumed that adopters could not be found for them, but we are convinced that if sufficient effort is made early, while the children are still very young, Negro as well as Asian babies can be given the security of an adoptive family.

Adoptive Applicants

The British Adoption Project has demonstrated that a considerable number of British families, both white and non-white, are interested in adopting children of minority or mixed race. The recruitment of applicants in the Project was very much easier than expected, and as more immigrants become established in steady employment and in adequate housing, it should be possible to find, not only white applicants, but also an increasing number of good homes of the same racial background as the children. However, agencies will need to be flexible in their requirements, and all who work with applicants, whether social workers or committee members, must be willing to search out and understand their own individual feelings about colour and race; otherwise these feelings will get in their way when they are considering applicants.

It may not be possible for hard-pressed agency workers to learn all they would like to know about the diverse cultures from which people have emigrated to Britain. Yet perhaps they could learn something about the background of the minority groups they are most often called upon to serve in their particular community, and about the extent to which the background culture of these people is being modified by their experience in Britain. It would be especially appropriate to know the customs concerning marriage and family life, the rearing of children, illegitimacy, foster care and adoption. Although our knowledge of other cultures is still very limited, we have mentioned in Chapters 3 and 4 some of the information that helped the Project team to understand and work with natural parents and adoptive applicants of different races. Perhaps this will be of some help to other agencies.

A study from information in the case files of all the couples who applied to adopt revealed few differences in *circumstances* between successful and unsuccessful applicants. The differences were not great enough to account for the fact that some went on to adopt while others withdrew or their applications were rejected. When applications had to be rejected it usually was for more subtle reasons. The most frequent reason for rejection was some serious problem of personality or mental health, which seemed to make it inadvisable to enter into the complicated relationships that are involved in adoption. Subjective judgements necessarily enter into adoption decisions and we found it hard to pinpoint the criteria on which these assessments should be based, but when we reviewed the files afterwards, we found that those who adopted had some qualities in common, which certainly had entered into the successful outcome of their application. Other applicants often had these qualities, too, or some of them, but they did not become adoptive parents for one or more of the reasons listed in Table 5.6 in Chapter 5.

Use of Groups in Adoption

Groups are coming to play an increasingly important role in adoption in many agencies and the Project used them at two different points in the adoption process. Pre-application group meetings proved a helpful and efficient way to explain to several couples at once what would be involved in an application and what kinds of babies were needing homes. These meetings also gave any couples who were ambivalent or clearly ineligible a chance to withdraw without further involvement with the agency.

After legal adoption, most of the parents welcomed the chance to meet again in groups of six to eight couples to discuss their common interests and concerns as parents of an adopted child. The question of how, when and what to tell the child about his natural parents and background – particularly why the mother had given up the child – was the subject of most general interest. Although the matter of the initial 'telling', and the need to expand this (even into adolescence) to meet the developing child's curiosity and search for identity, had been discussed when the application was studied, these subjects had taken on increased importance by the time the discussion groups were held. Some other topics were of special interest too: minor incidents of prejudice which they had met without undue distress; what could be expected from heredity and from environment; how they could help their adopted children to accept their racial heritage with pride and still grow up British. These meetings were particularly effective in bringing out feelings about the whole experience of adoption, and about themselves as adoptive parents.

We concluded from these groups, that both the adopters and staff learned most when the groups were small and essentially unstructured, and when a member of the staff provided just enough leadership to keep the discussion focused on experience and problems unique to adoption. It seems evident that such discussions can be very helpful, but they could never be expected to make up for a poor family study or put right a placement that should never have been made.

Between Placement and Court Hearing

Comments of the Project adopters presented us with a picture of the futility of 'welfare supervision' and the duplication of work by the adoption worker, the welfare supervisor and the guardian *ad litem* in the period between placement and the court hearing.

Adopters often need help during the period between placement and legal adoption, but due to the uncertainty of their position they nearly always are too fearful to admit any difficulties or to use any help that is offered. It is our impression that even the adoption worker, who has placed the child and already knows the family well, can only rarely be of much real help during this time, and that the child care officer who enters the situation at this point as the welfare supervisor cannot hope to do much more than fill in routine forms or 'have a cup of tea and admire the baby'.

The welfare supervisor's role is much clearer in third-party and direct placements, where she is likely to be the first social worker involved in the adoption, and it might be well if her function could be limited to supervision of these placements. If adoption agency registration required adequate standards, these agencies could be made responsible for finishing what they have started, i.e. make sure the placement is satisfactory, the natural parents' consent valid, and finally appear at the court hearing as the responsible agent. This would eliminate the guardian *ad litem*, as well as the welfare supervisor, from agency placements and leave them free to pursue their duties in third-party and independent placements where their work is essential.

The court hearing was viewed by most adopters as a severe let down. There appeared to be a need for some brief ceremony or procedure, some moment that was recognized as the time when the child became legally the child of the adopters. Possibly some judges would welcome this, too, as in uncomplicated cases they often seemed unsure of what they were expected to say or do beyond signing the Order.

At the End of the Project

The follow-up interviews at the end of the Project found nearly all the children and their adopters getting on very well indeed, with the children well integrated into these families. At this early age, boys were making an especially good adjustment to life in their adoptive families, and so were Negro and part-Negro children. Non-white adopters were proportionately somewhat better represented than whites in the group of families rated as doing exceptionally well with their adopted children. Families with a father employed in routine office work or skilled manual work were also proportionately well represented in the group of highly successful adoptive parents.

Our numbers were very small and the children still too young for us to draw conclusions about their adjustment, but possibly even these very tentative findings may encourage more people to consider adopting a Negro or part-Negro child, and some workers to be more confident in placing them. It also looks as though success with non-European children may not be confined to highly educated or professional people alone, and that adoption homes may, therefore, be available to a greater variety of children.

We believe the work of the Project has contributed to an improved climate for interracial adoption and also for finding homes among the minority races in Britain. At least the Project has focused attention on children of diverse racial backgrounds and what is involved in placing them. We feel that ways should be explored now for involving more people, and especially non-Europeans, in a continuous effort to recruit adoptive applicants for these children, giving particular attention to seeking families for West Indian and Anglo-West Indian children for whom the shortage of homes still appears to be acute.

A special agency for placement of coloured children does not seem necessary or desirable. These children are part of the British scene and we believe their needs should be met, as those of white children are, by community agencies, both statutory and voluntary. However, it might be well for agencies to have someone with special responsibility for this work, so that it will not get lost in the multifarious duties of a busy office, and so that homes can be found quickly before age and damaging experiences make adoption unlikely.

Most of all, we hope agencies will break down the isolation which hinders the spread of knowledge and skills in adoption and prevents these children and adopters from finding each other, unless they happen to be known to the same agency. The Adoption Resource Exchange is demonstrating one way that knowledge and skills can be shared throughout Britain, and that children can be placed even if the adopters happen to live in another part of the country.

ARE membership is growing and since the Exchange is firmly based on high standards of practice, it holds exceptional promise for bringing a large number of British adoption agencies together in a co-operative effort to solve the problem of adoption for non-white children. It has frequently been suggested that the Exchange should be extended to serve all children with special needs in adoption, and this now appears likely. Standards found worthy in placing some children almost certainly will be used for other children. Thus, it seems that concern over the problem of adoption for non-white children, and the co-operative efforts being made on their behalf, may cause agencies to take a new look at adoption practice with benefit to all the children who depend on these agencies for parents.

LIST OF MEMBER AGENCIES OF
THE ADOPTION RESOURCE EXCHANGE
ON MARCH 31, 1969

*Birmingham Children's Department.

Church of England Family Welfare Committee, Bradford, Yorks.

Crusade of Rescue.

Dorset Children's Department.

*Dr Barnardo's Homes.

East Suffolk Children's Department.

Glamorgan Children's Department.

*Guild of Service, Edinburgh.

*Independent Adoption Society (formerly Agnostics Adoption Society).

London Borough of Greenwich Children's Department.

London Borough of Hammersmith Children's Department.

London Borough of Hounslow Children's Department.

London Borough of Lewisham Children's Department.

London Borough of Tower Hamlets Children's Department.

Manchester Children's Department.

Northern Counties Adoption Society.

*Oxford City Children's Department.

St Albans Diocesan Council for Social Work.

Sheffield Children's Department.

*Somerset Children's Department.

* Founding Members.

N

LIST OF TABLES

			PAGE
2.	2.1.	Age of children at adoption placement	31
	2.2.	Racial background of children placed by project	34
	2.3.	Type of care babies received prior to adoption placement	36
3.	3.1.	Ethnic background and country of origin of mothers of 53 adopted children	45
	3.2.	Social class of mothers of 53 adopted children	47
	3.3.	Living arrangements of mothers of 53 adopted children	47
	3.4.	Time of decision as related to ethnic background of mother	49
	3.5.	Ethnic background and country of origin of natural fathers of 53 adopted children	51
	3.6.	Social class of 53 natural fathers	52
5.	5.1.	Race and previous parental status of 51 adoptive couples	85
	5.2.	Race and previous parental status of 77 unsuccessful applicants	85
	5.3.	Social class of 51 male adopters compared with their fathers	88
	5.4.	Length of marriage of successful and unsuccessful applicants	90
	5.5.	Number of children of present marriage (adopters and unsuccessful applicants)	91
	5.6.	Principal reasons for withdrawal and rejection of applications to adopt a child	94
9.	9.1.	Comparison of ratings on children in follow-up study	161
	9.2.	Comparison of ratings on adopters in follow-up study	161
10.	10.1.	Adoption Orders in the United Kingdom, 1966 (statutory and voluntary agency placements)	167
	10.2.	Adoption Orders, 1966, Divisions of United Kingdom (statutory and voluntary agency placements)	168
	10.3.	Adoption Orders, 1966, Standard Regions of England and Wales (statutory and voluntary agency placements)	168
	10.4.	Adoption Orders, 1966, Standard Regions of England and Wales (statutory agency placements only)	169
	10.5.	Adoption Orders, 1966, Standard Regions of England and Wales (voluntary adoption societies only)	169

10.6. Children adopted by foster parents, 1966   170

10.7. Percentage of adoptions by foster parents, 1966   170

10.8. Adoption Orders and children not offered for adoption (non-white children, 1966)   172

10.9. Non-white children needing adoption on the last day of the reporting year   173

10.10. Additional factors complicating adoption of non-white children needing adoption on last day of the year   175

N*

BIBLIOGRAPHY

ADDIS, R., *et al.*, *A Survey Based on Adoption Case Records*, National Association for Mental Health, London, 1955.

Adoptability, A Study of 100 Children in Foster Care, State Charities Aid Assoc., New York, 1960.

The Adopted Adult Discusses Adoption as a Life Experience, Lutheran Social Service of Minnesota, Minneapolis, USA, 1968 (mimeographed).

The Adoption of Negro Children: A Community-Wide Approach, Social Planning Council of Metropolitan Toronto, Canada, July 1966 (limited circulation).

Adoptions Involving Mixed Races, Report on a Study Day at Vaughn College, Leicester University, published by Standing Conference of Societies Registered for Adoption, 1968.

ANDREWS, ROBERTA G., 'Casework Methodology with Adoptive Applicant Couples,' *Child Welfare*, Vol. 42, No. 10, December 1963.

'Permanent Placement of Negro Children through Quasi-Adoption', *Child Welfare*, Vol. 47, No. 10, December 1968.

ANTROBUS, P., 'Coloured Children in Care: A Special Problem Group?', *Case Conference*, Vol. 11, No. 2, June 1964.

BAGLEY, CHRISTOPHER, 'Migration, Race and Mental Health', A Review of Some Recent Research, *Race*, Vol. IX, No. 3, January 1968.

BERNSTEIN, ROSE, 'Are We Still Stereotyping the Unmarried Mother?', *Social Work* (USA), Vol. 5, No. 3, July 1960.

BILLINGSLEY, ANDREW, *Black Families in White America*, Prentice-Hall, New York 1968.

BISKIND, SYLVIA E., 'Helping Adoptive Families Meet the Issues in Adoption', *Child Welfare*, Vol. 45, No. 3, March 1966.

BLOCK, JULIA B., 'The White Worker and the Negro Child in Psychotherapy', *Social Work* (USA), Vol. 13, No. 2, April 1968.

BLOOM, MURRAY TEIGH, 'Special Parents for Special Children', *Reader's Digest*, April 1962.

BORGATTA, EDGAR F., and FANSHEL, DAVID, *Behavioral Characteristics of Children Known to Psychiatric Outpatient Clinics (with special attention to adoption status, sex and age grouping)*, Child Welfare League of America, New York, 1965.

BRADLEY, TRUDY H., *An Exploration of Caseworkers' Perceptions of Adoptive Applicants*, Child Welfare League of America, New York, 1966.

BRAITHWAITE, E. R., *Paid Servant*, Bodley Head, London, 1962.

BRANHAM, ETHEL E., *Transracial Adoptions: When a Good Family is not Enough*, Los Angeles Bureau of Adoptions, 1968 (mimeographed).

BRENNER, RUTH, *A Follow-Up Study of Adoptive Families*, Child Adoption Research Committee, New York City, 1951.

BROWN, FLORENCE G., 'Services to Adoptive Parents after Legal Adoption', *Child Welfare*, July 1959.

CARLSON, PAUL V., *et al.*, 'Studies in Adoption', *American Journal of Orthopsychiatry*, Vol. 36, March 1966.

CHARNLEY, JEAN, *The Art of Child Placement*, University of Minnesota Press, 1955.

Child Welfare League of America Standards for Adoption Service (revised), Child Welfare League of America, New York, 1968.

Child Welfare League of America Standards for Services to Unmarried Parents, Child Welfare League of America, 1960.

COLLIER, CATHERINE R., and CAMPBELL, ANNE, 'A Post-Adoption Discussion Series', *Social Casework*, April 1960.

CONKLIN, LLOYD T., VIELBIG, JOHN A., and BLAKELY, THOMAS C., 'Use of Groups during the Adoptive Postplacement Period', *Social Work* (USA), April 1962.

DAVIES, JOHN W. D., 'Thursday's Child has Far to Go', *Case Conference*, Vol. 14, No. 8, December 1967.

DE HARTOG, JAN, *The Children*, Hamish Hamilton, London, 1969.

Deprivation of Maternal Care: A Reassessment of its Effects, Public Health Papers No. 14, World Health Organization, Geneva, 1962.

DINNAGE, ROSEMARY, 'Research on Adoption', *Case Conference*, Vol. 13, No. 10, February 1967.

EDWARDS, JANE, 'The Hard to Place Child', *Child Welfare*, Vol. 40, No. 4, April 1961.

ERIKSON, RIGMAR E., 'Counseling After Legal Adoption', *Child Welfare*, December 1961.

FANSHEL, DAVID, 'Indian Adoption Research Project', *Child Welfare*, November 1964.

    'Research in Child Welfare: A Critical Analysis', *Child Welfare*, December 1962.

    A Study in Negro Adoptions, Child Welfare League of America, New York, 1957.

FITZHERBERT, KATRIN, *West Indian Children in London*, G. Bell & Sons, London, 1967.

FRADKIN, HELEN and KRUGMAN, DOROTHY, 'A Program of Adoptive Placement for Infants Under 3 Months' (also discussion by Dr Ner Littner), *American Journal of Orthopsychiatry*, Vol. 26, July 1956.

FRICK, HARRIET, 'Interracial Adoption: The Little Revolution', *Social Work* (USA), Vol. 10, July 1956.

GALE, J. A. B., 'Non-European Children in Care', *Child Care*, 17, No. 4, 1963.

GEBER, MARCELLE, 'The Psycho-Motor Development of African Children in the First Year, and the Influence of Maternal Behavior', *Journal of Social Psychology*, No. 47, 1958.

GERARD, MARGARET W., and DUKETTE, RITA, 'Techniques for Preventing Separation Trauma in Child Placement', *American Journal of Orthopsychiatry*, Vol. 24, January 1954.

GLICKMAN, ESTHER, *Child Placement through Clinically Oriented Case Work*, Columbia University Press, New York, 1957.

GOCHROS, HARVEY L., 'A Study of the Caseworker-Adoptive Parenthood Relationship in Post Placement Services', *Child Welfare*, June 1967.

GOLDBERG, HARRIET L., and LLEWELLYN, H. LINDE, 'The Case for Subsidized Adoptions', *Child Welfare*, Vol. 48, No. 2, February 1969.

GOODACRE, IRIS, *Adoption Policy and Practice*, Allen & Unwin, London, 1966.

GOODMAN, ELIZABETH M., 'Habilitation of the Unwed Teenage Mother: An Interdisciplinary and Community Responsibility', *Child Welfare*, Vol. 47, No. 5, May 1968.

GOW, KATHLEEN M., 'Social Class and Social Work', *The Social Worker – Le Travailleur Social (Canada)*, Vol. 33, No. 4, October 1965.

GRAHAM, LLOYD, 'Children from Japan in American Adoptive Homes', *Casework Papers*, Family Service Association of America, New York, 1957.

GREBLER, ANNE MARIE, Adoption in European Countries', *Child Welfare*, Vol. 42, No. 10, December 1963.

Guide for Planning and Operating an Adoption Resource Exchange, Child Welfare League of America, January 1957.

HARRIS, DALE B., SCHAEFER, EARL S., FANSHEL, DAVID, COLVIN, RALPH W., and POLLOCK, JEANNE C., *Quantitative Approaches to Parent Selection*, Child Welfare League of America, New York, 1962.

HERZOG, ELIZABETH, 'Unmarried Mothers: Some Questions to be Answered and Some Answers to be Questioned', *Child Welfare*, Vol. 41, October 1962.

HOOPES, JANET L., *An Infant Rating Scale: Its Validation and Usefulness,* 1967.

HOWELL, ROBERT J., *et al.,* 'A Comparison of Test Scores for the 16–17 Year Age Group of Navaho Indian with Standard Scale (Arizona and New Mexico)', *Journal of Social Psychology,* No. 57, 1958.

JAHODA, GUSTAV, VENESS, THELMA, and PUSHKIN, I., 'Awareness of Ethnic Differences in Young Children', *Race,* Vol. 8, No. 1, July 1966.

JEHU, DEREK, 'Developmental Issues in Inter-Racial Adoption', *Case Conference,* Vol. 14, No. 9, January 1968.

KADUSHIN, ALFRED, *Child Welfare Services,* Macmillan, New York, 1967.
'Follow-up Study of Children who were Adopted when Older: Criteria of Success', *American Journal of Orthopsychiatry,* Vol. 37, April 1967.

KELLMER PRINGLE, M. L., *Adoption – Facts and Fallacies,* Longmans, London, 1966.

KINNIBRUGH, A. D., *The Social Background of Immigrant Children from Asia and Cyprus,* Occasional Paper No. 1, Institute of Education, University of Leeds.

KIRK, DAVID H., *Shared Fate,* Free Press of Glencoe, New York, 1964.

KNAPON, M. TH., 'Some Results of an Enquiry into the Influence of Child-Training Practices on the Development of Personality in a Bacongo Society', *Journal of Social Psychology,* No. 47, 1958.

KORNITZER, MARGARET, *Adoption and Family Life,* Putnam, London, 1968.

KORNITZER, MARGARET, and ROWE, JANE, *Some Casework Implications in the Study of Children Reclaimed or Returned before Final Adoption,* Standing Conference of Societies Registered for Adoption, May 1968 (mimeographed).

KRUGMAN, DOROTHY C., 'Reality in Adoption', *Child Welfare,* July 1964.

LAWDER, ELIZABETH, *et al., A Follow up Study of Adoptions;* Post Placement Functioning of Adoption Families, Child Welfare League of America, New York, 1969.

LITTNER, NER., *Some Traumatic effects of Separation and Placement,* Child Welfare League of America, 1956.

LUSK, JANET, 'Co-operation between Doctors and Social Workers in Adoption', *Child Adoption,* No. 53, 1968.

LYSLO, ARNOLD, 'Adoptive Placement of American Indian Children with Non-Indian Families', *Child Welfare,* May 1961.

MAAS, HENRY S. (Editor), *Perspectives on Adoption Research,* Child Welfare League of America, New York, 1965.

MAAS, HENRY S., 'The Successful Adoptive Parent Applicant', *Social Work,* V, No. 1, 1960.

MCWHINNIE, ALEXINA, *Adopted Children: How They Grow Up*, Routledge & Kegan Paul, London, 1967.

'Group Counselling with 78 Adoptive Families', *Case Conference*, Vol. 14, Nos. 11 and 12, March and April 1968.

MALMQUIST, CARL P., *et al.*, 'Personality Characteristics of Women with Repeated Illegitimacies: Descriptive Aspects', *American Journal of Orthopsychiatry*, Vol. 36, April 1966.

MARMOR, JUDD, 'Psychodynamic Aspects of Transracial Adoptions', *Social Work Practice*, National Conference on Social Welfare, USA, 1964.

MASSARIK, FRED., and FRANKLIN, DAVID S., *Adoption of Children with Medical Conditions*, Children's Home Society of California, Los Angeles, 1967 (mimeographed).

MENLOVE, FRANCES LEE, 'Aggressive Symptoms in Emotionally Disturbed Adopted Children', *Child Development*, Vol. 36, No. 2, June 1965.

MEYER, HENRY J., KRONICK, JANE C., HERZOG, ELIZABETH, and LEWIS, HYLAN, *Research Perspectives on the Unmarried Mother*, Child Welfare League of America, New York, 1962.

MORLAND, KENNETH, 'A Comparison of Race Awareness in Northern and Southern Children', *American Journal of Orthopsychiatry*, Vol. 36, January 1966.

NORRIS, MIRIAM, and WALLACE, BARBARA (Editors), *The Known and Unknown in Child Welfare Research*, Child Welfare League of America, 1965.

O'ROURKE, HELEN, and CHAVERS, FAY, 'The Use of Groups with Unmarried Mothers to Facilitate Casework', *Child Welfare*, Vol. 47, No. 1, January 1968.

Pamy's Progress, Report of recruitment campaign conducted by Parents-to-Adopt-Minority-Youngsters (PAMY), Centennial Building, St Paul, Minnesota (USA), June 1963.

PARKER, ROY A., 'The Basis of Research in Adoption', *Case Conference*, Vol. 10, No. 4, September 1963.

PATTERSON, SHEILA, *Dark Strangers*, Tavistock Publications, London, 1963.

A Political and Economic (PEP) Report on Racial Discrimination, Research Services Ltd, London, 1968.

Pregnancy in Adolescence, Report of a Conference, March 10, 1966, sponsored by NCUMC, London.

PRICE, JOHN REA, 'West Indian Immigrants: Assimilation and Casework', *Case Conference*, Vol. 12, No. 2, June 1965.

RATHBUN, CONSTANCE, MCLAUGHLIN, HELEN, BENNETT, CHESTER, and GARLAND, JAMES A., 'Later Adjustment of Children Following Radical Separation from Family and Culture', *American Journal of Orthopsychiatry*, Vol. 35, April 1965.

RAYNOR, LOIS, 'Interracial Adoption in Britain', *Social Work* (USA), Vol. 14, No. 2, April 1969.

RIBBLE, MARGARET, *The Rights of Infants*, Columbia University Press, New York, 2nd Edition, 1965.

ROSE, E. J. B., and Associates, *Colour and Citizenship: A Report on British Race Relations*, Oxford University Press, London, 1969.

ROSNER, GERTRUDE, *Crisis of Self-Doubt*, Child Welfare League of America, New York, 1961.

ROWAN, MATILLE, PANNER, REUBEN, and EVANS, BYRON W., *Casework with the Unmarried Father*, three articles reprinted from *Child Welfare*, revised 1968.

ROWE, JANE, *Parents, Children and Adoption: A Handbook for Adoption Workers*, Routledge & Kegan Paul, London, 1966.

SANDGRUND, GERTRUDE, 'Group Counselling with Adoptive Families after Legal Adoption', *Child Welfare*, June 1962.

SANTS, H. J., 'Genealogical Bewilderment in Children with Substitute Parents', *British Journal of Medical Psychology*, Vol. 37, No. 2, 1964.

SCHAPIRO, MICHAEL, *A Study of Adoption Practice, Vol. 1: Adoption Agencies and the Children They Serve; Vol. 2: Selected Scientific Papers; Vol. 3: Adoption of Children with Special Needs*, Child Welfare League of America, 1956.

SELLERS, MARTHA G., 'Transracial Adoption', *Child Welfare*, Vol. 68, No. 6, June 1969.

SHAPIRO, PAULINE, 'Some Illegitimate Coloured Children in Long-Term Care', *Case Conference*, Vol. 15, No. 1, May 1968.

SHAW, JULIE A., 'Following up Adoptions', *British Journal of Psychiatric Social Work*, No. 8, November 1953.

SKODAK, MARIE, and SKEELS, HAROLD, 'A Final Follow-up Study of 100 Adopted Children', *Journal of Genetic Psychology*, Vol. 75, 1949.

SMITH, BRENDA, 'Finding Foster Homes for Pre-Adoption Babies', *Case Conference*, Vol. 13, No. 7, November 1966.

SMITH, I. EVELYN, *Readings in Adoption*, Philosophical Library, New York, 1963.

SENCE, ROSALIE, 'The Assessment of Children who have been Boarded-Out with a View to Adoption', *Child Care Quarterly Review*, Vol. 14, No. 3, July, 1960.

STONE, F. H., 'Adoption and Identity', *Child Adoption*, No. 58, 1969.

SUZUKI, RYO, and HORN, MARILYN, *Follow-up Study of Negro-White Adoptions*, Los Angeles Bureau of Adoptions, Los Angeles, California, 1968 (mimeographed).

SWAN, CLARA, 'Adoption Resource Exchange in New York State', *Child Welfare*, Vol. 35, November 1956.

TAYLOR, ANN, 'Institutionalized Infants' Concept Formation Reality, *American Journal of Orthopsychiatry*, Vol. 38, No. 1, 1968.

TEC, LEON, and GORDON, SUSANNE, 'The Adopted Child's Adaptation to Adolescence', *American Journal of Orthopsychiatry*, Vol. 37, March 1967.

THEIS, VAN S. SOPHIE, 'How Foster Children turn Out', State Charities Aid Association, New York, 1924.

TRISELIOTIS, JOHN, 'Courts and Adoption Practice', *Case Conference*, Vol. 15, No. 5, September 1968.

'The Timing of the Single Mother's Decision in Relation to Adoption Agency Practice', *Child Adoption*, No. 58, 1969.

Unmarried Mothers: Their Medical and Social Needs, Standing Conference of Societies Registered for Adoption, London, 1968.

The Use of Predictive Methods in Social Work, National Institute for Social Work Training, London, April 1967.

VALK, MARGARET A., *Korean-American Children in American Adoptive Homes*, Child Welfare League of America, 1957.

VINCENT, CLARK E., *Unmarried Mothers*, The Free Press, New York, 1961.

WILSON, ANDERSON C., *Policy and Procedure for the Operation of the Adoption Resource Exchange*, Mimeographed Bulletin No. 11, Office for Children and Youth, Department of Public Welfare, Harrisburg, Pa (USA), 1961.

WIMPERIS, VIRGINIA, *The Unmarried Mother and Her Child*, Allen & Unwin, London, 1960.

WINNICOTT, DONALD, *The Child and the Family*, Tavistock Publications, London, 1957.

The Child and the Outside World, Tavistock Publications, London, 1957.

WITMER, HELEN, et al., *Independent Adoptions: A Follow-up Study*, Russell Sage Foundation, New York, 1963.

YARROW, LEON, 'Separation from Parents in Early Childhood', Chapter 2 of *Review of Child Development Research*, edited by Martin L. Hoffman and Lois W. Hoffman, Vol. I, Russell Sage Foundation, New York, 1964.

YELLOLY, MARGARET A., 'The Mother's Decision', *Sociological Review*, Vol. 13, No. 1, March, 1965. Reprinted in *Child Adoption*, No. 49, 1966.

INDEX

Accommodation
of adoptive applicants 79, 89
of mothers at time of conception
46–7
reason for mother reclaiming baby
56
Adjustment
of Project children at follow-up
160–5
Adolescence 20, 140, 147, 148, 165
Adoptability
children not offered for adoption
171–2
definition of 30
deterrents to 174
health problems as factor in 38–9
limitations imposed by research
30
and ratio of adopters to children
58
Adopted Children
curiosity about origins 20, 114,
115, 189
feeling about own colour 140,
156
identification with adoptive
parents 115
sensitive to criticism 157
studies of 103, 115, 151–2, 162
Adoption Act 1958
and agency responsibility for
child 107
committee responsibilities 65,
100
opportunity for mother to change
her mind 47, 123
See also: Consents
Adoption Agencies
administrative requirements 81

and ARE 179, 193
difficulties in finding homes for
coloured children 24
lack of communication between
32, 33, 178
policy in regard to rejections 72
premature disclosure of information about babies 108
regulations deterring non-white
applicants 176
religious requirements 80, 187
responsibility if consent general
107
special agency for coloured children not needed 191
success in placing non-white children 166–76
Adoption Resource Exchange 9,
21, 28–9, 61, 178–84, 191–2
Adoptive applicants
characteristics of 81–94
children of 69–70, 91, 114, 128
desirable attributes in 59
discouraged by 'red tape' 81
motivation of 66, 68, 163
of other races 27, 76–81
positive qualities found in the
successful 96–8
preparation of for adoptive parenthood 74–5
reasons for withdrawal or rejection 94
recruitment of 58, 64, 188
See also: Childlessness; Group
meetings; Health; Medical services; Placement; Rejection;
Working mothers
Adoptive parents
adjustment to parenthood 121

Adoptive parents (*contd.*)
   attitudes to illegitimacy 68
   difficulty in using 'welfare super-
      vision' 121
   fear of mother's change of mind
      122–3
   feelings about child's colour 144–
      5, 157
   feeling of difference towards
      adopted child 144
   need to accept child's background
      109
   other children born to 157
   patterns of family life 157
   ratings at follow-up 159–65
   and timing of placement 121–2
   See also: Adoptive applicants;
      Group meetings; Reclaims by
      natural mothers
African
   responsibilities of children to
      parents 140
   wish for a similar child 80
Age
   of adoptive applicants 86
   of child and response of adoptive
      parents 144
   gap at placement 69, 91
   importance of early placement
      34–5
   preferences of applicants 92
   of Project children at placement
      30–1, 35
Appointments 64, 125–6
Asian
   adjustment of Asian children at
      follow-up 164
   attitudes to illegitimacy 44
   baby girls easily placed 34,
      187
Assessment
   versus education for adoptive
      parenthood 74

Attitudes to Adoption
   of Asians, Africans and West
      Indians 27, 54
   of caseworkers 33, 66–7, 97, 187
   of relatives of adoptive applicants
      71–2
   See also: Grandparents

Background of child
   adoptive parents' feelings about
      109, 140–2
   getting and giving information
      about 108–10
   interpretation of 'bad' 175
   sharing with others 140
Bedford College 9, 19, 23–5
Bernard, Dr Viola 66
Boarding Out with a View to Adop-
   tion
   See: Fostering
Bradley, Trudy 97
Bramall, Margaret 42
Brenner, Ruth 103

Case Committees 24, 65, 73, 100,
   104
Casework
   with adoptive applicants 64–81,
      120–4
   with children 69, 111–12
   with natural parents 27, 32–3,
      41, 56
   See also: Caseworker; Interviews;
      Placement
Caseworker
   cast in role by client 54
   and clients of other races 76–81
   and interracial adoption 19, 33,
      66, 68, 97
   need to be aware of own feelings
      187–8
   need to be present at placement
      113

Caseworker (*contd.*)
  See also: Casework; Colour; Interviews; Prejudice
Charnley, Jean 112
Child Care Officer
  as Guardian *ad litem* 119
  as 'welfare supervisor' 124–7, 190
Child Welfare League of America
  39, 79, 109
Childlessness 67, 81, 137, 139, 149
Children of Adoptive Applicants
  69–70, 91, 114, 123, 128, 147, 157
Church of England Committee for Diocesan Moral and Social Welfare Councils 166
Colour
  caseworker's feelings about 33, 68, 77, 187
  child's feelings about his own 140–1, 156
  difficulty in finding acceptable words for 21
  effect on child's adjustment 144
  implications for 'telling' 139–41
  importance of to immigrant adopters 80, 102
  and neighbourhood in relation to adoption applications 89–90
  public comment in interracial placements 142–3
  white adopters' feelings about 144–5, 155, 163
Confidentiality 114
Consents
  law in relation to 30, 47–9, 123
  possibility of general consent 107
  Project arrangements for obtaining 30, 104–5
  Timing of 48–50, 104–6, 186
Coordinating Service
  See: Adoption Resource Exchange

Court Hearings 127–30, 190
Criteria for Prediction 26, 63–4, 74, 83
Cultural Differences
  adopted child's heritage of 141
  in attitudes to illegitimacy 44–6, 54
  in decision about adoption 56, 186
  need for greater understanding of 186
  significance in adoption applications 76–81
  See also: Colour; Interracial adoption; Religion

Decision of mothers for Adoption 48–9, 55–6, 105–6
Difference
  adopted child's feelings about 140
  caseworker's attitudes to 97
  coloured child's recognition of 140, 151
  in feelings of adopters to child 144, 148–9
  racial and cultural in adoption applications 76
Dinnage, Rosemary 98
Discipline 157
Discussion Groups
  See: Group Meetings

Early Placement 31, 34, 103, 146
Education
  of adoptive applicants 87
  of natural fathers 52
  of natural mothers 46
Emotional Problems
  in adoptive applicants 94–5
  in child 39

Fanshel, Professor David 84, 88,
    151–2, 165, 197
Fathers
    See: Adoptive Parents; Natural
    Fathers
Fitzherbert, Katrin 45
Follow-up Study
    method 152
    plans for 20, 28, 165
    purpose 151
    results 154–65
Forms 65, 81, 122, 180
Foster Homes
    as meeting place 110–11
    Project children's experience in
    35–6
    See also: Fostering; Foster mothers
Foster Mothers
    adopters' feelings about 146
    need for news of baby 120
    at placement 110–13
    See also: Foster Homes; Fostering
Fostering
    as means of adoption 97–8,
    169–71, 185
    compared with adoption 41, 56,
    115
    need for research 171, 185–6
    See also: Foster homes; Foster
    mothers

Goodacre, Iris 131
Grandparents
    influence on natural mother's
    decision 50, 55
    interviews with adoptive grand-
    parents 71–2
    reactions of adoptive grand-
    parents 143, 148, 156
    West Indian 46
Great Ormond Street, Hospital for
    Sick Children 37
Greek Orthodox Religion 43–4

Grochos, Harvey L. 131
Group Meetings
    post adoption 75, 122, 131–50,
    189–90
    pre-application 61–4, 145, 189
    use in follow-up study 20
Guardian *ad litem* 119, 124–7, 190
Guyana 32, 44, 45
    See also: West Indian

Handicapped Children 30, 39, 97,
    174–6, 183
Hard-to-place Children
    See: Handicapped children
Health
    of adoptive applicants 70, 71, 86
    of children 30, 37–40, 121, 154
    complicating factor in placement
    175
Heredity 141
Hernias 39
Hindu
    See: Illegitimacy; Religion
Home Study
    adopters' reaction to 145–6
    Project methods in 61–81
    See also: Casework; Interviews
Hong Kong Project 23, 59, 85
Houghton Committee 9
Housing
    See: Accommodation
Hurst Committee 95

Illegitimacy
    attitudes of adopters to 68
    attitudes of immigrants to 44–6,
    54
Indian
    See Asian
Infertility
    establishment of 81
    See also: Childlessness

Institutional Care
  See: Nurseries
International Social Service   10, 19,
  23, 24–5, 179
Interracial adoption
  comparison with intraracial   26,
    151–3
  implications for 'telling'   139
  need for longitudinal study of
    151–2
  special qualities needed for   96–7
  study of American Indian children
    in white American homes   151
  See also: Colour
Interviews
  with adoptive applicants   64–9
  with applicants of other races   76–
    81
  with children of applicants   69
  combined with group meetings
    149
  in follow-up study   153
  importance of first   34, 64–5
  with referees and relatives   71–2
  See also: Casework; Caseworker;
    Rejection

Judges
  at court hearing   127–30
  interpretation of 'unreasonable'
    123

Kellmer Pringle, Dr M. L.   57
King, Mary   25
Kirk, H. David,   74, 109
Kornitzer, Margaret   152

Law
  See: Adoption Act 1958; Con-
    sents; Court Hearing; Guardian
    ad litem; Supervision
Legal Complications
  as bar to early placement   175

Liaison Service
  See: Adoption Resource Exchange

Maas, Henry S.   88
Marginal Applicants   83, 97
Marmor, Dr Judd   97
Marriage
  effect of arranged marriage on
    adoption plans   45, 50
  length of in adoption applicants
    90
  West Indian attitudes to   78
Matching   100–104
McWhinnie, Dr Alexina   150
Medical Problems
  See: Health
Medical Services
  assessment of applicants   70–1
  examination of babies   37–9
  See also: Health
Meeting of Mothers and Adopters
  42, 114–18, 146
Mothers
  See: Natural Mothers
Motivation   66, 68, 163
Muslim
  attitudes to illegitimacy   43–4
  attitudes to women   80
  customs about names   78
  See also: Religion

Names   77–8, 122
Natural Fathers
  attitudes to baby   54
  casework with   32, 42, 53–4, 187
  characteristics of   50–3
  consents from   105
  custody of child   105
  See also: Colour; Cultural differ-
    ences
Natural Mothers
  attitudes of officials to   33
  casework with   27, 32, 41, 56
  characteristics of   42–50

Natural mothers (*contd.*)
  individual needs of   42, 54
  special problems of with mixed
    race child   23
  wish for information about adop-
    ters   105
  See also: Consents; Cultural
    differences; Meetings with
    adopters
Negro
  adoptive applicants   80–1
  children at follow-up   164, 188,
    191
  children placed by Project   34,
    37, 182, 188
  study of Negro applicants by
    Fanshel 81, 84
  See also: Cultural differences
Newspapers
  See: Publicity
Numbers of Non-white Children
  adopted in Britain in 1966   167–
    71
  needing placement   171–6
  placed by Project   27
  referred to Project   31
Nurseries   35–6, 111, 146, 155

Pakistani
  See: Asian
Personality of Child   102, 103, 144,
    158
Photographs   42
Pittsburgh Study of Negro Appli-
    cants   81, 84
Placement
  adopters' feelings about methods
    146
  meeting of mothers and adopters
    42, 114–18, 146
  meeting places   110–11
  methods   107–14
  selection of home for child   100–4

Pre-adoption fostering   35–6, 38
Prediction   26, 74, 83–4
Prejudice
  in adoptive applicants   68
  in caseworkers   68, 77–81
  preparation of child for   148
Publicity   59–61, 86
Putative Fathers
  See: Natural fathers

Questionnaires   22, 152–4, 166–7

Race
  adopted child's feelings about
    140
  caseworker's attitudes to   19, 68–
    9, 76–81
  of children in Project   34
  confused with nationality   32
  as factor in selection of home
    101–2
  importance of accuracy about   32,
    185
  See also: Colour; Cultural dif-
    ferences; Natural fathers and
    mothers
Racial Discrimination
  adopters' experience of   138–48,
    158
  effect on applicants   76–7
Rating Scale   158–9
Reclaim of Children by Natural
    Mothers
  adopters' fear of   121–3
  effect on adoptive family   147
  judge's attitude to   123
  Project experience of   48, 56,
    123–4
  and timing of consents   30
  See also: Consents; Natural
    Mothers
Recruitment of Adopters   58–61,
    182, 188, 191

References 72
Register
  See: Adoption Resource Ex-
    change
Registration of Adoption Agencies
  190
Rejection of Applicants 64–5, 72–
  4, 94–5, 189
Relatives 71–2, 143, 156
  See also: Grandparents
Religion
  of adoption applicants 86
  and adoption planning 43–4, 80,
    187
  advice to adopters by CCO 125
  agency requirements about 80,
    187
  court inquiries about 129
  of immigrant adopters 79–80
  of natural parents 43, 52, 187
Research
  Bedford College help with 19,
    23
  characteristics of adoptive appli-
    cants 83–98, 188–9
  comparison groups 26–7, 164–
    5
  criteria for prediction 26, 74,
    83–4
  follow-up study, methods of 152–
    4
  into size of problem 166–76,
    185–6
  limitation of small numbers 26,
    191
  need for in foster home adoptions
    171, 185–6
  plans for continuing 28, 152,
    165
Ribble, Dr Margaret 36
Robertson, James and Joyce 37
Role of Adoptive Parents 65, 66,
  73, 74–5

Rowe, Jane 109, 160
Second-child Applications 75–6
Shaw, Lulie 144
Sikh 78
  See also: Cultural differences;
    Religion
Social Class
  of adoptive applicants 87–9
  of natural fathers 52
  of natural mothers 47
  related to mother's decision 49–
    50
  and success of adoption 163–5
Standards 180–1, 183–4
Standing Conference of Societies
    Registered for Adoption 1967
    study 76
Success in Adoption
  and criteria for prediction 26,
    83
  difficulty in measuring 26, 171
  ratings of Project placings 158–
    65
Supervision
  adopters' difficulty in using 121–
    2, 131
  difficulties of present arrange-
    ments 124–7, 190
  legal requirements 119
  need for flexible period 122
  Project responsibility for 120
  See also: Guardian *ad litem*
Telling 139–40, 149–50, 152
Temperament
  See: Personality
Temporary Care 186–7
Time
  cultural differences in attitudes to
    77
Timing
  of adoption applications 95
  of adoption placements 111, 121

Timing (*contd.*)
  of post-adoption groups   132
  of 'welfare supervision' visits
    125

University Department
  cooperation with social agency
    19
  effect on recruitment of adopters
    59
Unmarried Mothers
  See: Natural Mothers

Welfare Supervision
  See: Supervision

West Indian
  attitudes to illegitimacy   44–6
  attitudes to marriage   78
  needs to recruit homes for   61,
    188
  understanding of adoption   56
  working wives   78
  See also: Colour; Cultural dif-
    ferences; Negro
Withdrawal of Adoptive Applica-
    tion   81, 84, 94–5
  See also: Rejection
Witmer, Helen   162
Working Wives   78–9, 156

Yelloly, Margaret   48–50

GEORGE ALLEN & UNWIN LTD

Head office:
40 Museum Street, London, W.C.1
Telephone: 01-405 8577

Sales, Distribution and Accounts Departments
Park Lane, Hemel Hempstead, Herts.
Telephone: 0442 3244

Athens: 7 Stadiou Street, Athens 125
Auckland: P.O. Box 36013, Northcote, Auckland 9
Barbados: P.O. Box 222, Bridgetown
Beirut: Deeb Building, Jeanne d'Arc Street
Bombay: 103/5 Fort Street, Bombay 1
Calcutta: 285J Bepin Behari Ganguli Street, Calcutta 12
P.O. Box 2314 Joubert Park, Johannesburg, South Africa
Dacca: Alico Building, 18 Motijheel, Dacca 2
Delhi: B 1/18 Asaf Ali Road, New Delhi 1
Ibadan: P.O. Box 62
Karachi: Karachi Chambers, McLeod Road
Lahore: 22 Falettis' Hotel, Egerton Road
Madras: 2/18 Mount Road, Madras 2
Manila: P.O. Box 157, Quezon City, D-502
Mexico: Liberia Britanica, S.A. Separos Rendor 125, Mexico 4DF
Nairobi: P.O. Box 30583
Ontario: 2330 Midland Avenue, Agincourt
Rio de Janeiro: Caixa Postal 2537-Zc-00
Singapore: 248c–6 Orchard Road, Singapore 9
Sydney: N.S.W.: Bradbury House, 55 York Street
Tokyo: C.P.O. Box 1728, Tokyo 100-91

Also in the series

ADOPTION POLICY AND PRACTICE

IRIS GOODACRE

'. . . a sympathetic and expert exposition of the work and responsibilities of those employed to arrange adoptions.'   *The Guardian*

'For the student there is invaluable reference throughout to reports, royal commissions and Acts of Parliament, and there is a summary of the legal background. . . . This book hits exactly the right note: a clear statement of an investigation along with examples that bring out the emotional strains inherent in adoption as a practical measure.'   *New Society*

'. . . an important addition to the sparse literature on adoption.'
Family Planning

'Everyone working in adoption will do the job better for reading the book.'   *Welfare*

National Institute For Social Work Training Series, No. 9 Demy 8vo 212 pages

CHILD CARE: NEEDS AND NUMBERS

JEAN PACKMAN

In her comprehensive survey, which takes into account a wide sample of children from all over England and Wales, Dr Packman discusses in detail the problem of children in the care of local authorities.

'This is an important, well written and fascinating book.'
Child Care Quarterly Review

National Institute for Social Work Training Series No. 15 Demy 8vo 248 pages

LONDON: GEORGE ALLEN AND UNWIN LTD